WOW
Woman Of Worth

Women in Business
in a Changing World

Christine Awram

Published by Inspire Higher Consulting Inc. May 2021
ISBN: 9781777109059

Editor: Danielle Anderson
Typeset: Tara Eymundson
Book Cover Design: Judith Mazari

CONTENTS

Women in Business in a Changing World
is dedicated to all the audacious
women who have embraced entrepreneurship.
We have been faced with extraordinary challenges over the
past 18 months, in a world that constantly changes.
You have risen to these challenges with
grit and determination.
This book is a testament to your tenacity and
courage, and we salute you.

The Wow Credo

I am a Woman Of Worth
My worthiness is inherent and infinite –
    it is my natural state
My value is a reflection of who I AM –
    and I am magnificent
Who I am always makes a difference –
    because I MATTER
I am successful –
    coming from my true power which lies within
I am empowered –
    making choices from the clarity of my heart, mind and
    spirit
I am an empowered leader –
    impacting others from quiet acts of kindness to
    leading a nation
I am abundant –
    manifesting success from my core values
I cherish my relationships –
    they are part of what makes me strong
I am a Human BEing –
    as my BEing is of far more significance than my
    DOing
I play, laugh, and bring beauty and light into the world –
    I am RADIANT
At times I despair and I weep –
    when I feel the pain of a world that has momentarily
    gone mad
Yet even when I tremble through a dark night of the soul,
    I renew my faith and my courage in a single heartbeat
    because my spirit is indomitable
I feel, and I care, and I am passionately alive –
    with a heart as open as the universe

I AM A WOMAN OF WORTH, AND I AM GLORIOUS

"A Taste of WOW" – Your FREE Book is Waiting

This eBook includes eight chapters:
one from each book in the original WOW Series,
to give you a taste of the
powerful and heartfelt writing of our authors.
Topics include Moms in Business,
Empowered Entrepreneurs, The Power of Collaboration,
Life & Leadership with Soul, Aging With Moxie,
Mental Health Matters,
Thriving Through Turbulent Times, and Pandemic!

Get your free copy of
"A Taste of WOW" here:

www.awomanofworth.com/books

Acknowledgements

This entire book could be filled with the names of all the people I want to thank, for the many ways you've all helped inspire this book to become a reality. Heartfelt gratitude to the tremendous community I call my WOW Tribe. You rock.

To the fabulous females who are this book's contributing authors, you have staggered me with your willingness to show up 100%. Each and every one of you share my burning desire to make our world a more joyful and empowered place, and you've been the most courageous and extraordinary women to collaborate with. It has been an honour.

To my publisher Julie Salisbury, for taking my hand every step of the way while sharing your brilliance and making this adventure fun. You shine a very bright light my friend.

To our brilliant editor Danielle Anderson, you put all the pieces together to make our books shine even brighter. And to our graphic designer Judith Mazari, your book cover designs are a work of art.

To my family and closest friends, you are the inner circle of my Tribe. I have no words to express how grateful I am for your love, and that you always have my back.

And especially to David Samuelson, my beloved Manly Man. You always believe in me, and see the best in me. I couldn't have done this without your love, faith and support. You are my heart.

Contents

Introduction

By Christine Awram, Founder
Woman Of Worth WOW Worldwide

*"In order to change ourselves,
we must first believe we can."*
Marie Forleo, Everything is Figureoutable

Introduction

By Christine Awram, Founder

It was one o'clock in the morning, and after waking from a restless sleep, I reached for the glass of water that sat on my nightstand. Damn, it was empty. Still half asleep, I debated if I should get up. Then I realized that I also needed to pee, so the decision was made.

Instead of using the upstairs bathroom like I normally would, I found myself heading downstairs to get some filtered water. I've since asked myself why water quality was so important in the middle of the night, given the consequences.

At the top of the stairs, my left foot slipped out from under me and rapidly headed downwards, along with the rest of my body. However, my right foot stubbornly tried to remain exactly where it was. Something bent in a direction that it was never anatomically meant to, there was a bolt of excruciating pain, and I shrieked in agony while tumbling helplessly down the stairs.

My brain fogged out a little, but I found myself sprawled on the landing screaming F-bombs with tears streaming down my face. I admit to being a complete wimp when it comes to pain, so I wasn't being stoic about it. There was a thump from above as my poor husband came running, having been jolted awake from a dead sleep. He somehow managed to half carry half drag me the rest of the way downstairs. I demanded to be put on the toilet immediately – even with the unbelievable pain I was experiencing, I still needed to pee!

After icing, elevating, and medicating (the pharmaceutical kind, along with arnica and other natural anti-inflammatories), we decided it was likely a really bad sprain. There were no bones sticking out of my skin, the painkillers were doing their job, and with COVID-19 cases seriously escalating due to the third wave of the pandemic, I had zero interest in going to a hospital unless it was life-threatening. My amazing husband (affectionately known as Manly Man) set up a cot downstairs and proceeded to take great care of me.

The pain was still rather awful over the next few days, but my foot seemed to be slowly healing. However, I started to sense that something wasn't quite right, so I went for x-rays. Sure enough, I had a broken ankle. The lab immediately sent me off to the ER, which was completely different than pre-pandemic and reminded me of a scene from the movie Contagion. But the staff were amazing, and I do mean seriously amazing. I knew they were all operating on fumes, exhausted and emotionally drained, but they were still incredibly caring and compassionate throughout. Respect.

I ended up with a plaster cast and was sent home with strict instructions to elevate my leg and stay off my foot for the next four weeks. After a year of pandemic isolation, I was now basically immobile.

At this point you may be asking, why am I sharing this personal story in a book about women in business in a changing world? Well, I've shared a number of different stories in the previous eight books in our Woman Of Worth series, including some of the ways that I've pivoted my business along with my mindset during Covid, and almost every change I've made has required considerable action. Now I found myself being asked to shift yet again, and I wasn't sure what I had left. After some deep soul-searching, I made a decision that I knew wouldn't come naturally to me at all.

I decided to do … nothing.

Even through the fog of painkillers, I could hear an inner voice whispering to me. *Hey Christine, how about if you just rest for a while? It won't be a vacation, but still, take a break. Plant your ass in that recliner, keep your leg elevated just like the doctor recommended, read some books, watch some tube, take some naps. Chillax.*

I've learned to have faith in my inner voice, so even with my logical mind hating the idea, "nothing" is exactly what I decided to do.

It's not something that I would have previously advised, and I'm not saying that doing nothing is always a wise decision – my butt has grown a couple sizes as a result – but I trust my intuition. Having built a strong network over the years, the world kept turning as my amazing tribe helped out both personally and professionally – especially my fabulous publisher and editor with this book! Manly Man created wonderful meals every single day, and he even man-cleaned with only minor grumbling.

At the time of this writing, it's been almost two months

since I fell down the stairs and all is well. I'm now out of the plaster cast and into an Aircast. It turns out that the plaster one wasn't set quite right, so it caused soft tissue damage throughout the time I was wearing it. This damage would have been so much worse if I hadn't made the choice to stop moving and do nothing!

This latest episode in my rather eventful life reinforced the core foundation of my success and happiness: listen to your gut, and always trust your intuition. Our inner voice is the greatest source of wisdom and most accurate compass we'll ever have, so long as we allow ourselves to be quiet enough to hear it.

In this moment, I also can't help but reflect on the fact that a broken bone, once properly healed, is even stronger than it was before. And this process is true for so many different aspects of our lives. A marriage ends or a loved one dies, leaving us heartbroken and unsure of our future. An injury occurs that forever changes the way we interact with the world. A business is forced to close, a home is lost, a terrible secret is revealed. There are so many obstacles that can crash up against us, fracturing us in ways we don't expect. But what matters is not that we were broken; what matters is that we heal. Our world changes, and we change with it, finding new ways to follow our dreams and become even more of who we are meant to be.

In this ever-changing world, there are so many ways to shift, pivot, and adapt. Our most recent books have naturally focused on COVID-19 and the way people have responded to it, but change has always been a part of life and will continue to be for the rest of time. Our authors talk about the many ways they successfully transformed or grew their businesses after facing a myriad of obstacles – not only the pandemic but also health issues, divorce, finances, and more. Some stories focus on the inner journey, sharing how your mindset can help you conquer challenges and become unstoppable; others provide more practical steps, describing the ways they pivoted their own business as a source of inspiration. There are stories of finding your own self-worth, of stepping into your feminine power, of learning to let go of control, of getting back up every time life knocks you down. There is something profoundly meaningful for each and every person in this book.

All our authors have a common denominator, which is a belief that anyone can do anything. By sharing their deeply authentic stories, they hope to inspire you to believe the same. They'll reach into your heart as well as your mind and open you up to endless possibilities. For anyone who might be feeling somewhat broken and battered by life's changes and challenges, take a deep breath and know that your strongest self is still before you. You've got this.

"Don't go against your inner knowing.
Just don't.
Trust yourself."
Maria Erving

About Christine Awram

Christine Awram, founder of Woman Of Worth WOW Worldwide is a bestselling author, dynamic speaker, visionary, and philanthropist. Christine radiates vitality with her indomitable spirit, yet her earlier years began as a teenage runaway who experienced addiction, illness, and depression. She inspires others by sharing stories about how she moved from futility to fulfillment, and transformed challenges into passion and purpose – usually with a good dose of irreverence and her trademark humour.

Christine's commitment to the empowered leadership of women resulted in her being honoured with the Outstanding Leadership Award by the Global Women's Summit. She has personally inspired thousands of women through her WOW events and programs, and has published nine #1 bestselling books in just three years. She is also part of the bestseller *Pursuit:365* along with such luminaries as Jann Arden and Bif Naked.

"Everyone has a story that matters, and everyone's story is someone else's road map. The beliefs you shifted to overcome challenges, the grief you survived, the fears you faced down, the courageous decisions you made . . . other women need to learn and be inspired by you. They need to know that it can be done."

www.aWomanOfWorth.com
Facebook: @aWomanOfWorthWOW • **Instagram:** wowWofW
LinkedIn: WOW Christine Awram • **Twitter:** @womanofworthwow

Foreword

By Shelly Lynn Hughes, Publisher
Fresh Magazine

*"Alone we can do so little,
together we can do so much."*
Helen Keller

Foreword

By Shelly Lynn Hughes

In many of our stories, we create heroes who are solely responsible for solving whatever problem society is facing. In reality, though, the idea that a single individual has the answer is ludicrous. No one person can save the world — but *together*, we can. We need each other to find answers, get things done, and push society forward.

True collaboration is subtle and complex, and the leaders in this space are doing a few things differently from the fictional heroes of our stories. Heroes see everyone as a competitor or a follower; collaborative leaders need other people and invite them to lean in and elevate one another until everyone achieves and wins. For instance, interdependent leaders set community-oriented and seemingly impossible goals like "achieve equality" or "end homelessness." The nature of these goals requires collaboration.

This concept does not just apply to society at large. If you have something amazing – a product, an idea, a concept – then the bigger it gets, the harder it is to hold onto on your own. As it grows further, you may need more and more people to help you. For that product to become a brand, that idea to become a program, and that concept to become a movement, you need collaboration. It is the antithesis of ego and the drive behind all great things. To achieve this greatness, everyone at the table must have a voice, and everyone contributes. When we authentically collaborate, we share the credit, the blame, the wins, and the losses.

In my own experience, each company I have founded or owned has been collaborative in nature. Media, publishing, skincare, crowdfunding, speaker series, and author – in each of these areas of business, I would not have succeeded to the degree I have experienced without the collaborative efforts of my teams, the women around me, and the people who believed in my vision.

Recently, I had the opportunity to elevate the voices of 365 Canadian women in my published book, *Pursuit:365*, launched in the midst of a pandemic to bring hope, excitement, and humanity to a national audience. There would have been no way to achieve this landmark accomplishment if I had not approached it as an entirely collaborative project. Coming off a huge pivot and cancelling a planned speaker series nation-wide, I turned to my team with the desire to find another way to give some of these voices a platform. With my experience in publishing, having owned a magazine for over a decade, the idea of a collaborative book with exciting co-authors seemed fantastic! If I only knew then what I know now.

We launched in headfirst, piecing together the project and inviting our first authors to the table. They didn't just accept, they leaped at the opportunity to participate. We sold out in just over a month, but our work had only just begun. To cut to the message of my story, we had a core team of about five individuals who were tasked with bringing this project to fruition, but if you asked me who worked with me on this, I would tell you approximately 400 people were involved. That's a lot of people! We had a lot of wins; we also had a few setbacks. If it had been just the core team working on this project, those setbacks would have been massive for each of us – especially for me. What made it work was the strength of our team and the collaborative spirit that each and every person authentically adopted throughout the process.

It's the same here. Being a Woman Of Worth is all about the value we each bring to our community. It is about elevating the voices of the women around us. It is about sharing our stories, finding ourselves in the stories of others, and continuing to do so because it is *valuable*. Because it has *worth*.

Women have a unique relationship with the concept of collaboration. Looking back through history, in every corner of the Earth it has always been women who are the drivers of cooperation. Communities are centred around women, built by women, and brought together by women, yet the work we put in to maintaining those communities has often gone unnoticed or unappreciated. But the world is changing. We live in the most globally connected world that has ever existed, which means we have seemingly unlimited opportunity for connection and progress. The women of today are ready to share our voices with readers and listeners everywhere in new and inventive ways.

"Real queens fix each other's crowns," or however the phrase goes. The way the world is changing. It's not just about what you or I can do, it's about what we can do together to be bigger, better, stronger.

When you go through this book, take note of the true value that these women have chosen to share with you – like all truly collaborative leaders, there is a community-oriented and impossibly enormous goal at play. WOW was created to fulfill the goal of profoundly impacting and celebrating the spirit, success, equality, and empowered leadership of all women. If you share in this goal, then here is your call to action! Take this as an invitation not just to consume the voices of the select few phenomenal women featured here, but also to share your own voice. Take to social media, call a friend, submit a story to a local publication, share what *you* have to say. On behalf of women, I invite you to share your voice the way we are sharing ours here.

About Shelly Lynn Hughes

Shelly Lynn Hughes is the founder of Fresh Magazine, a partner in Skin Spin Cosmetics, Project Her Inc, and YOYOMAMA.CA, and the creator of the Amazon bestselling book, *Pursuit:365*.

In addition to her work as a publisher and business owner, she has developed an exclusive skincare label for a major pharmacy and consulted for various magazines and health and beauty brands. Shelly was also awarded the prestigious WOW Woman Of Worth "Mom Entrepreneur of the Year" Award in 2013.

She loves to get her hands on an idea, make it a reality, and share it with the world – all while radiating the good vibes of a best girlfriend.

www.freshmag.ca • www.skinspin.com
www.yoyomama.ca • www.projecther.com
Twitter: @iamshellylynn
Instagram: @shellylynn.hughes

1

Enjoy the Journey

By Tiffany-Ann Bottcher

*"There will come a point in everyone's life,
however, where only intuition can make the leap
ahead without ever knowing precisely how.
One can never know why
but one must accept intuition as fact."*
Albert Einstein

Enjoy the Journey

By Tiffany-Ann Bottcher

My life has been an incredible journey full of highs, lows, and everything in between. I am still young, just thirty-four, but I have already done a lot of "living." In my mid-twenties I dove into personal development, which has given me incredible clarity about who I am and where I want to be. I am 100% Type A. I am analytical and logical. I have a deep-rooted need for practicality that doesn't intuitively align with my decision to leave my long-term, well-paid, stable corporate job mid-pandemic. Yup, that's right. While unemployment is high and the economy is weak, I decided to take the biggest leap of faith in my life.

When I reflect on everything that has happened in the last decade, it feels pretty remarkable. In the span of just ten years, I have finished my undergraduate degree and then a graduate degree, been married twice, divorced once, had three kids, gone through countless health issues including IVF and an emergency hysterectomy – oh, and pursued a serious climb up the corporate ladder. It has been an adventure!

While my inner perfectionist would love to tell you that this has all been easy and I have loved every minute of it, that wouldn't be truthful. And while being vulnerable isn't something I enjoy, I have come to realize that this is an area where I must continue to grow. Being a mom has provided me insight into an entirely different mindset. I often consider what would happen if one of my kids sat across from me one day and told me a story much like my own. What would I think? What would my advice be?

Well, my advice would be to always enjoy the journey of life. If you aren't enjoying what you are doing, make a change! It is easy to fall into the "next" trap – living for the next vacation, next sunny day, next free moment – but the truth is, sometimes there is no "next."

When I was seventeen, I was involved in a motor vehicle accident that changed the course of my entire life. Up until that moment, I'd had everything planned out: I wanted to develop my equestrian career and was already doing a significant amount of coaching, competing, and training. I had big dreams of competing internationally, and it consumed my entire life. I put all my eggs in one basket and refused to listen to anyone who told me this was a bad idea. If you are going to be the best at anything, you have to have this level of passion and commitment. However, this means that if things don't work out, it can create a pretty serious identity crisis.

Looking back now, I know that I kept pushing when my body was clearly telling me to stop. My intuition knew my equestrian career was over, but I ignored it. I tried to outwork the pain, continuing to ride for at least a year longer than I should have. In the end, I was forced to recognize that I just couldn't do the same things anymore. My body told me what my intuition had been telling me for quite a while now: it was time for some change.

When I came to the realization that my future was going to be different than what I had imagined, I took all of my competitive drive and put it elsewhere. I started rebuilding my life in a new direction and went back to school for my business degree. I made some great choices and some terrible ones too. Realistically, I was starting a new life with a whole group of new people; thankfully, my intuition is an amazing judge of character. And yet I would often feel myself reasoning with it, thinking to myself "if things have not changed by such-and-such date, then I will move on," or "that person was just having a bad day, it will get better." My intuition knew the way, but more often than not, I ignored it.

I don't regret my choices – each of them aided me in becoming the person I am today – but I would say that there were times when I could have taken an easier path. And while my intuition was usually loud, my ability to speak up when I needed to was severely lacking.

As someone who had grown up in a barn, spending more time with horses than people, navigating what seemed like a new world had its challenges. To go back to school, I needed a well-paid night job. I delivered pizza for a while, then got a job serving drinks at a dive bar forty minutes from my house. I learned a lot about people and how to speak up while working there, which was not something I expected.

Climbing the corporate ladder was an adventure all on its own, especially in a male-dominated industry. There were a few women, always ambitious, and it felt like there was an intense level of competition between us. It was as if there was an unspoken rule that there was only room for one at the top. Unfortunately, this scarcity mindset only worked to our disadvantage. Rather than rise together, the women crawled over each other, which ultimately undermined the efforts of all involved. As I watched many talented colleagues come and go, I started to really notice the negative side of ultra-competitive ambition. I often felt very misunderstood – my ambition and drive combined with my introverted, type A personality was often confused with being cold, uptight, and intimidating. I knew I wanted to create a positive change but didn't really know how.

I attended my very first conference specifically for women in 2019, and it was eye-opening. I found the outlook on the differences between men and women to be fascinating. Often, we spend so much time trying to prove we are equal that we forget to acknowledge there are distinct differences between the sexes. Women and men communicate differently, and since most of my coaches and mentors had been male, I had never learned how to navigate these differences. Using some of the knowledge I gained from this conference, I focused on improving my communication and people skills. However, I found learning in a real-time business setting to be very unforgiving, with few people in my immediate circle willing to provide constructive feedback. This process was very frustrating for me – I wanted to learn and improve, and I felt like I wasn't progressing.

I was very fortunate to be a part of a corporate organization that valued innovation and gave me space to grow and evolve as a person and leader. I jumped into every role, project, or challenge with a passion for excellence. If I needed to learn something, I dedicated myself to the task. I wanted the team to win, I expected from others what I expected from myself, and I wasn't afraid to get my hands dirty. While I was growing personally, the organization was growing as well. Year after year, we experienced massive growth in revenue as well as team size. When I started, I was one of five employees; towards the end of my tenure, staffing was up in the mid-eighties.

I love to learn and continued to grow in every way I could. I continued my education, read books, worked with coaches and mentors, and travelled to amazing conferences. I just wanted to be the best I could be, no matter what game we were playing. I cultivated skills in task management and automation, business optimization, change implementation, and strategic planning.

But as the years continued on, that nagging intuition returned. It told me that I had more to offer the world, and that it was time for another change.

Have you ever felt like you are in a fight with yourself? Like your intuition loves to say "I told you so"? That is where I was at. The more I learned about the leader I wanted to be, the more I knew I needed change. My heart was no longer in my work; each day felt transactional. The nagging feeling that something was out of place was relentless, and I battled with it for well over a year.

I can do anything if I can envision it in my mind. I remember when I was on a trip to Las Vegas and decided I was going to jump off the Stratosphere, which is an 829-foot guided free fall from the top of the tallest building on the strip. I remember playing it out in my mind, overthinking each piece not because I was too afraid to do it, but because I needed to be able to envision the process. Leaving my job was beginning to feel like this jump. I couldn't see the way forward; I couldn't envision the process. I began to feel angry at myself. I was smarter than this, and my intuition knew the way. I knew the destination – I had notebooks full of ideas for a consulting firm that would use my skills to help scale businesses for passionate entrepreneurs. I wanted to build my own business, and my intuition was my biggest cheerleader. However, it just didn't seem like a practical idea. I couldn't see how to get there.

I pressed on in my corporate role, but my mindset was in an ugly place. Each time my health deteriorated, a different doctor would say, "This seems stress-related. Are you stressed?" I would always respond with "no more than usual," which was true! I had just learned to live in a chronic state of stress. It turns out that skin irritation, digestive problems, hearing issues, body pain, anxiety, depression, insomnia, exhaustion, and weight gain can all be stress-related. And my stress was really coming from a single place: my fight with my own intuition.

I knew I needed to make sense of it all. So, I developed the "Significant Six" method of evaluating my life. This identified six significant parts of my life that needed to live harmoniously. I don't mean they all must be given an equal focus; I mean that I need to make conscious decisions about each of these areas. If you are going to "ride the line," you better be paying attention, and it was clear I was riding the line with my health. In fact, I am a habitual line rider, completely ignoring one or more parts of my life while pouring everything I have into another. When I was about twenty years old, I was working graveyard shifts at a fast-food joint, going to school, and training multiple horses each day. I slept for a few hours on alternating evenings. In short sprints, these types of sacrifices can make the difference between an average life and an amazing one. That being said, sustaining these choices for any amount of time never ends well. By creating a framework to work off of, I was able to use the logical and analytical part of my brain to bring understanding and focus to the evaluation of my life. Here are my "Significant Six":

- Financial: Income, savings, debt load, money management, and any stress and wellbeing associated with these items.
- Relational: Partners, family, friends, children, anyone you carry an ongoing relationship with or wish you had a relationship with.
- Creative: Soul-feeding activities that are not income based. Some examples could be crafting, reading, hiking, or meditating – the passion projects.
- Professional: Your career or business. Typically these are income-generating, but not always. This activity provides fulfillment and growth.
- Emotional: The ability to manage emotions, thoughts, and feelings.
- Physical: The physical body and its functions. This can include movement, fitness, and/or physical health.

Each week, I assessed these areas on a scale of one to five, then added them all up to create a total score. As an analytical person, this numerical reference allowed me to create a tangible evaluation of my life.

When I first created this framework, my life looked incredible on a surface level. I was earning a salary that was in the top 5% of Canadians, I had an amazing family, and I was very fortunate to be living the life I had dreamed of. I had everything I thought I wanted, yet I couldn't get a score over eighteen out of the potential thirty no matter how hard I tried.

My health was terrible. I wasn't the mom or wife I wanted to be. Managing my emotions was becoming a challenge. The long inner struggle was taking its toll. I tracked my score for weeks and there were definite fluctuations, but I knew that eighteen wasn't a good representation of the life I wanted to lead.

My intuition was getting harder to ignore – in fact, many days it was practically yelling at me. Each time something negative would happen, I would have an inner conversation of "I told you so." So, with no real plan and no overthinking, I decided to listen to my intuition and leave my job behind. After years of climbing the corporate ladder, I realized that I had been climbing the wrong one. As a careful planner and strategist, this realization was humbling, terrifying, and liberating.

There is making a decision, and then there is actually implementing it. Those around me were shocked, not because I wanted to do something different but because as much as I had been battling this internally for a long time, I hadn't shared any of it. I quickly realized that if you are going to take an out-of-character leap, you need to be ready for people to give you a well-intentioned talking to. Humans like to be safe and staying was a safe choice. I know anyone who tried to discourage my jump meant well, but I had enough confidence in my decision to press on and create my own business consulting firm.

My journey is just getting started, but I have a renewed energy and excitement. I have committed to 2021 being the healthiest year of my life, I am in the early stages of my new business, and I am showing up as the person I want to be for my husband and kids. I still ride the line, but I am paying attention to the Significant Six, making conscious decisions, and trusting the strength and wisdom of my intuition. I feel a sense of peace and clarity; the state of unrest and inner struggle is over.

As I navigate these major changes in my life, I am reminded to enjoy the journey. My mom wrote this message at the end of every note and card when I was a kid, and while I didn't truly understand it then, I do now. There will still be highs and lows and everything in between, but now, with my new mindset, I know that I will enjoy the ride.

About Tiffany-Ann Bottcher

Tiffany-Ann Bottcher has spent nearly a decade in corporate finance and technology, learning and refining what works, what doesn't, what's needed most, and why. A full-time business coach, blogger, MBA student, wife, and mother of three, Tiffany-Ann believes that technology and people working together can accomplish nearly anything and create a values-based, people-first culture.

Career stops include financial controller focusing on key data metrics and building processes; director of operations guiding revenue growth and team performance; VP of corporate development, leading acquisitions, mergers, and systems development; and VP of finance and technology, unleashing growth in systems, integration, automation, and optimization.

Beyond such admirable business experience, Tiffany-Ann is most proud of her three amazing kids, Sophie, Parker, and Kane, and the life of adventure she shares with her husband Jarred. Their journey is ongoingly chronicled in her hugely popular blog "The Mom Who Wants it All."

To inquire about coaching, consulting, or to learn of upcoming events, contact Tiffany-Ann at links below. You can also visit her website to complete your Significant Six evaluation.

www.tiffanyannbottcher.com
Facebook: @tiffanyannbottcherconsultant
Instagram: @momwhowantsitall

2

A Leap of Courage

By Shelina Mawani

"When you focus on hurt, you will continue to suffer. If you focus on the lesson, you will continue to grow."
Author Unknown

A Leap of Courage

By Shelina Mawani

When you look at me today, you would think my journey to success was a straight path, clear of demanding challenges and obstructions. However, to say that was the case wouldn't be genuine. My pilgrimage towards prosperity and happiness in the business world has been a long one, and it has been met with several hardships along the way.

I was born in Mwanza – a city in northern Tanzania, East Africa – where I grew up without computers, cell phones, TV, large shopping malls, and many of the conveniences we have today. I was a carefree small-town girl just living day by day, unsure of what my long-term goals or vision would be, especially after failing my senior year of high school. One fine evening, after I came home from evening prayers, my brother asked me about my plans for the future, and I replied that I wanted to take a secretarial course. I made this decision not because I was interested in this course, but because all of my peers were going to the city of Dar es Salam for their studies and I didn't want to be left alone. With that, I went off and completed my secretarial course, then came back to Mwanza and worked for a few years.

Then, when I was twenty, I had my "aha" moment. My parents have always had a lot of compassion for the less fortunate, and that has had a huge impact on me. One day, my mother forced me to drive the nuns back to the church with their groceries. A storm had rolled in so it was raining heavily as we arrived, thunder rumbling and lightening flashing across the sky. I saw children with leprosy walking towards the gate to get the groceries we had brought, and I froze in shock, tears rolling down my cheeks. This was when I first became aware of this deadly disease, the poverty experienced by those afflicted with it, and their living conditions. In that moment, I became passionate about being part of the solution.

I decided to become an ambassador for leprosy. In my first project, I landed myself the role of youngest chairperson for the Lioness Club of Mwanza, an internationally affiliated organization dedicated to helping communities through charitable causes. For one of my projects, I was able to set up diagnostic camps for locals to create some much-needed awareness about leprosy. The other project I assisted in was sending eight children to England to receive treatment for their heart murmurs, which was not available to them in East Africa.

Due to unrest in Africa, my brother sponsored us to move to Canada in 1982 so that we could enjoy a stable and safe life. Here we were embraced and accepted as citizens. I got married in 1985 and had two sons, the first born in 1987 and the second in 1992. Then, when they were very young, I lost my job and decided to embark on a journey into the world of entrepreneurship. My sister Nasim was also in need of work, so we opened a 700-square-foot restaurant in Burnaby.

Without the support of my children and my husband, I would never have been able to start this business. It was a difficult time in many ways. Nawaz worked fourteen-hour days to support our family and also helped me financially in my day-to-day business. My children grew up on their own, with the older brother looking after the younger one. I drove a 1968 Pontiac Parisienne which I had paid $250 for, with doors that did not lock and wipers that did not work. My eldest had to become an expert in guiding me to see through the rain-streaked windshield.

After nine months in operation, Nasim and I had to close the doors of our restaurant as it was losing too much money. Instead, we decided to transition to the wholesale samosa market. There was an increasing demand for ethnic foods and samosas were being sold in mom-and-pop stores all over the area – this was a food that we had grown up with and loved, so we thought we could make an impact in the market. With that, Nana's Kitchen was born. Our first factory space was only 1,700 square feet, allowing us to produce between 400-1,000 samosas per day. We started selling them to small coffee shops, gas stations, universities, and pizza shops as grab-and-go items.

When we were first looking at creating our product, we considered what we could do to stand out. Initially, I thought it would be about taste. We looked outside the box and created an amazing gourmet product that stood out from the traditional Punjabi samosa that was commonly available. We used a completely different pastry and taste profile, and our samosas were over three times the size of our competitors. However, we soon realized that our current market was not a good target for our product. I had to face the fact that price was a barrier in the ethnic community, and so the bigger picture of selling to the mainstream community through grocery retail was born. We established our brand as a gourmet product, and in 2001 we acquired our first major grocery retailer. One would think that this was the happy ending to my story and the key to my success. However, I am reminded of the expression "be careful what you pray for because you might get it."

Getting the business of a large grocery chain was a joy, but it came with its own burden. This meant we had to move from our small facility with a staff of ten to a custom-built HACCP-approved plant that required more than doubling our team. This also meant getting federal inspectors on site each day to check that we were following good manufacturing practices and confirm all our export declarations. We spent almost three years upgrading our facility. Our staff all had to be FOODSAFE and WHMIS-certified and go through a vigorous training process before they could even step into the production area.

Today I am proud that we are the only HACCP/BRC-certified plant producing samosas in British Columbia. However, when I look back at the huge investment it took to reach this goal and the failures I experienced along the way, I count myself lucky that I have made it. We had a much higher chance of failing than succeeding; I should have done my research about the finances that were required before we jumped into this new direction. The costs of building this new facility and training all the staff were high – almost instantly, we had a 1424% increase in operational expenses and a 690% increase in rent just to maintain our current sales volume. I maxed out my line of credit and was then forced to take out a second mortgage on my family home and borrow from my relatives. Then, in 2008, the recession hit and the economic toll of my debt grew heavy.

One morning, my bank called and told me, "You are a risk for our business. Your line of credit is used too much, and we consider your business to be an unworthy partner." Then, the man made me an offer – or as I saw it, took us hostage: "Pay us $25,000.00, and then we will send a risk assessment advisor to look at your plant operations and your administration. If you do that, we can remain your bank." I was totally shattered; it felt as if this would be the end of my business. I could not afford to close as I had too much at stake, but there were too many hurdles to continue. Fortunately, I found another bank, Envision Financial, that was willing to take on my business and the outstanding loan without the risk assessment. This allowed us to keep operating, but nothing changed about my everyday struggle to come out of my financial stress. My accounts were always overdrawn, and I would sit on the stairs every night and cry as I tried to figure out what would I tell the bank next morning. Needless to say, times were tough. I was paralyzed by the fear of rejection.

There were five long, hard years where our sales did not meet our overhead. During this time, I got really good at juggling our income and expenses. Sometimes this required a call to the bank, *pleading* with them not to bounce our rent cheque. "Just give us two more days" became my slogan. There were times I couldn't afford to pay my employees and had to ask them to push their paycheque back one or two weeks. I couldn't pay the bills, and our vendors were ready to put our account on hold. For those who have never experienced financial difficulty, it's hard to explain the deterioration of your mind and emotions. It's like your consciousness is stuck in one place, and the negativity that surrounds you buries any instincts and judgments you have left. You cannot think about what's going to happen tomorrow because you're too busy worrying about how to get out of your current situation.

I could not have gotten through this time or seen the success that I have today without my employees – it is because of them that I am now a successful entrepreneur. As an immigrant and a woman of ethnicity, I understand firsthand the struggles that come with immigrating to a new country. This fuelled my passion to create opportunities for people from different ethnicities and backgrounds. I hired people with little to no English and gave them an opportunity to thrive and gain confidence. Today, these same employees are still with us and are now in management positions. With teamwork, we can achieve the extraordinary.

At the end of those five years, we finally saw the light at the end of the tunnel. The lease on our factory was paid out, and Nawaz, who had joined the business in 2002, had developed our Canadian market and had started to penetrate the US market as well. This was a huge turning point for us and Nawaz was the one who made it happen, travelling for weeks at a time to establish brokers and distributors. And yet all I could see was that I was still stuck in a room that was on fire. Then, I ignited the spark within me and took the leap to change my thinking. I felt a new beginning coming towards me and welcomed it with open arms. But in order to meet this new beginning, I had to change my mindset and re-evaluate the whole situation. I had to take on a positive outlook and convince myself that even though I was drowning in debt, I could do what it took to come out of it. By this time, I had learned a very important lesson: that I had to drown before I could swim. This truly became an asset for me. Everything was in the midst of deep change, and

I knew that the roads were going to be rocky. I could not let my fear betray my worth.

To truly succeed, I decided that we needed to improve our execution and marketing. We hired a consultant on a contract basis to help us brand our product as well as identify and overcome our weaknesses. We also hired right-minded personnel who were professionals in marketing, social media, trade shows, and brokering to take our business to the next level. Finally, we brought on a volunteer board of advisors made up of people who had owned large corporations, and they were able to help guide us through some of our business decisions.

Throughout my professional career, I have developed a personal philosophy that offers solutions to the problems that surface in the midst of creating a business. I call them my "three C's." The first C is **conversation**, which holds significant value in the business world. When you encounter a problem, no matter how far-reaching it may be, conversation is your biggest asset. One of the ways I raised awareness about our products is that I started to network on social media and advertise at community events. I did product demonstrations at local stores, spoke at local colleges and universities, and attended events where I could have a table to display my flyers and share what makes my product different from any other in the market. These all allowed me to communicate directly with our customers and ensure that our product met their expectations.

The next C is **collaboration**. Regardless of your strengths, you will fail to achieve your goals in business without collective collaboration. While you must first believe in yourself and your product, you will also need to ask for advice from those with experience in the field and be willing to use their help to take your business to the next level. Personally, I joined women's organizations that would meet every month so I could network with like-minded women and get some solutions to my problems.

The final C is **celebration**, and it remains a pivotal component of my journey to success. You must always remember to celebrate every win, no matter how small. In the beginning I would forget to celebrate because I was so focused on my struggles and failures, but now I celebrate every milestone because they demonstrate that everything has entwined together to create a business built on love and respect. And thankfully, we have lots of reasons to celebrate! Today, Nana's Kitchen occupies an over 30,000 square foot facility in the heart of Surrey, BC, and produces more than 30,000 handmade samosas each day, which are sold in grocery stores throughout North America, even as far as Hawaii and Alaska. In my time as a businesswoman, I have won many prestigious awards, including Business Woman of the Year by Times of Canada and Best Export Business by Surrey Board of Trade, both in 2016. In 2017 I won "woman of the decade" through the Women Economic Forum, and in 2018 I was the only Canadian woman awarded the Bharat Saman award by the House of Lords in London, England. In 2019, I was recognized by Bank of Montreal for community and charitable giving. And in 2020, I won the 44-plus resilience category through the Surrey Board of Trade and Nana's Kitchen was voted as being in the top 11 for women-owned businesses in British Columbia by Business in Vancouver.

With all that being said, my mindset is always about giving more and expecting less. Throughout my life, I have continued to make positive impacts on the people around me wherever I can. I was on the organizing committee for Salama Gala, which raised funds for Camp Good Time for kids suffering from cancer and also supported the Watoto wa Africa orphanage in my homeland of Tanzania. Most recently, my business has become a community champion for Surrey Memorial Foundation, local food banks, and local community programs.

To me, courage is not about changing or grasping for something better – it is about being in the present. I was able to overcome the constraints of living in a third world country and the struggles of immigrating to a faraway, unknown place. I then pushed through the challenges of starting and expanding a business to become the Samosa Queen, as I have been dubbed by customers and friends. And now, my newest passion is speaking about my journey of embracing failures to achieve success.

There are many lessons that I hope you will take from my story. One is that even the most successful entrepreneurs have made mistakes along the way, and this has allowed them to discover valuable lessons that enable their growth. So, regardless of the market you enter, be sure to do your homework. Don't fool yourself into thinking that things will just fall into place, and make sure you have the funds to support your business ventures in the long term. Also, remember to question whether your product or service is in demand and ensure that you're considering both passion and practicality.

Another crucial lesson has been the importance of family. My husband, Nawaz Mawani, and my children, Samir and Sarfaraz, are my biggest inspirations and have supported me throughout this entire journey. Without them, I would not be where I am today.

Finally, make sure you dream big but also have realistic goals. Take a few minutes every day to reflect on your goals and achievements and make sure you are on track for where you want to be. To make the leap in your mind, you have to possess the right mindset. And when you orientate your goals to embrace conversation, collaboration, and celebration, there's no telling what you can achieve.

There were some very hard years during my journey to success, and living through them was no easy feat. However, I have learned so much from my failures that today, I salute them. My happiness was always within me, and to find it, I just had to seize the moment. Honour your scars, as they have made you who you are today. My mission in life is just not to survive but to thrive with passion and style, and that is a right for every human being – including you.

www.yournanaskitchen.com
Email: smawani@yournanaskitchen.com
LinkedIn: Shelina Mawani • **Facebook:** Shelina Mawani
Instagram: @shelinamawani • **Twitter:** @mawanishelina

About Shelina Mawani

Shelina Mawani is a resilient and successful businesswoman. Affectionally known as the "Samosa Queen," Shelina is the visionary behind Nana's Kitchen, a multi-million-dollar company producing gourmet handmade samosas in Surrey, British Columbia.

Success did not always come easy for Shelina. Born in the small town of Mwanza, Tanzania, she grew up without a formal education or long-term goals for the future. She moved to Canada in 1983 and faced a series of setbacks, including a failed restaurant business. Undeterred, Shelina kept her entrepreneurial spirit alive. Through a combination of embracing struggles, celebrating successes, and collaborating with others, Shelina had the strength and enthusiasm to succeed. Following in her parents' footsteps, she dedicates her time to helping others and is now able to employ and mentor more than fifty new immigrants to Canada.

Shelina has earned many awards and recognition over the years, including being listed as one of the top 11 women-owned businesses in BC by Business in Vancouver and winning the business resilience award for the 41-plus category by the Surrey Board of Trade. She attributes her success to the lessons she learned throughout her journey, along with the amazing support of her family.

3

Pivot, Not Panic

By Amy Andersen

*"You have everything you need to build
something far bigger than yourself.
The people around you realize this, and they
are ready to follow if you're ready to lead."*

Seth Godin

Pivot, Not Panic

By Amy Andersen

For many of us, 2020 started with a bang. On March 21, all personal service industry businesses in British Columbia, Canada were shut down indefinitely – and I was one of them. I had just spent over $10,000 to sponsor two major events in Chilliwack, and I wouldn't see one cent of return on that investment. Great. In addition to my now-closed salon being my only source of income, I was also in the middle of an expensive divorce. And, since I am self-employed, I was unable to postpone or hold any payments such as my mortgage, credit cards, or bills. The federal and provincial government had set up programs that helped many people, but it seemed I wasn't going to be receiving anything from them. I had to figure out what to do, and fast.

I certainly couldn't have predicted any of this when I first opened my sugaring salon on September 1, 2013. I had been a single mom for the last few years after my husband and I divorced in 2010, and I was on the hunt for a new career. I had just left a job working in a medical call centre as I didn't make enough to cover daycare, preschool, and after school care for my children. I decided I needed to find something that both paid the bills and allowed me to work from home. My parents were very supportive and volunteered to watch my kids one day a week, but my mom hadn't yet retired so she couldn't offer full-time care. So, I also needed to find something that could work around my children's schedule with their father, my mom's babysitting availability, and my kids' nap schedules/bedtimes. This should be easy, right?

A long-time friend of mine who had a sugaring salon in Abbotsford had been asking me to come work with her for years. With no other options in sight, I finally picked up the phone and called her. I wasn't sure what exactly I would do, but if she was willing to work around my weird schedule, I was more than willing to take her up on her offer. After three months of working a few hours here and there, she had taught me the basics of both body sugaring and running a salon. The plan was that I would create my own sugaring salon in my home, and then we would both refer customers to each other and help each other when we could. I converted a rec room into an office/waiting area and attached a shower curtain to a dowel I hung from the wall to create a treatment area. That September, I held the grand opening for Just Peachy and had over 100 clients in my first month of business.

Hard work, determination, and support from friends and family allowed me to grow my business over the following three and a half years to the point where I needed a larger facility. I sold my townhouse and purchased a home in an area of Chilliwack I had always wanted to live, which was within walking distance of my boys' elementary school. My salon was still located in my home, but now it was more than twice the size with two treatment rooms, giving me the ability to hire staff. I brought on my first staff member in the summer of 2016, and I finally was able to make more and work less. My dream was starting to become reality.

For the next few years, I worked harder than I ever had before as I juggled my clients, the business, my now multiple staff, and my family life. By the end of 2019 I had 3,000 annual clients and five staff members; the salon was open almost twelve hours a day, seven days a week; and I had incorporated the business. I was making more money than I ever thought imaginable, and Just Peachy was becoming a household name throughout the city. Everything was working out better than I had ever planned, and I expected exponential growth in 2020.

This year, which I now refer to as "the year that shall not be named," started out rough. My second husband and I had just separated and I was grieving the loss of my father and uncle, both of whom had passed away from cancer. I turned my focus entirely to my business, believing that it was the only area in which I had total control – I was about to find out how wrong I was! The first weekend in March, Just Peachy sponsored two major women's events in Chilliwack, BC: the Fraser Valley Women's Expo and the International Women's Day put on by the Chilliwack Chamber of Commerce. We spent over $10,000 in advertising and promotions, and we had put more work into the 2020 trade show than ever before. I was confident I would see results, both in the number of new clients coming to the salon and in financial growth. However, there were already the first stirrings of concern about this new virus that had hit China, and then Italy. I watched the news more than I ever had in my life, and yet I still did not expect the announcement that came from Dr. Bonnie Henry on March 21. I made an Instagram post letting our clients know that their upcoming appointments would most likely not happen, but that we fully anticipated to be open long before April 1. How naïve I was!

With the exception of my father and uncle's recent illnesses, my family and I were healthy people. My medical record indicates that I had chickenpox when I was six years old, but neither my mother nor I remember it. I've never broken a bone in my body, and the only times I was ever in the hospital was to birth my two children and get my hysterectomy. I did not expect Covid to affect us. And yet every day my bank account got lower, my pile of bills got higher, and the sense of dread deep inside me got larger.

I had done the math, and I was seriously worried that if we were not allowed to open the salon back up by June 15, I would lose both my income and my house. Not only would my children and I be devastatingly affected by the worldwide pandemic known as COVID-19, but so would my staff as this was their families' only source of income as well. But I wasn't willing to just give up. I had worked too hard for too long to watch my dream go down the drain. I was not going to be defeated by a virus I hadn't even seen the effects of yet. I was not going to roll over and become a statistic. I was going to fight, and that meant I had to come up with a new plan.

For the first four years that my salon was open, I was the only sugaring salon in Chilliwack. During that time, clients of mine started to comment that they loved my business and were envious of the fact I could work around my kids' schedules. "Why don't you open a sugaring salon too?" I would ask them. "I will train you! I will help you! It will be great! When we are too busy to fit clients in, I will refer them to you." My friend in

Abbotsford and I had kept up this arrangement for the last few years, but having another sugaring salon in Chilliwack would be way more convenient for my clients. I also wanted to help some fellow single moms out the way I had been helped in the beginning. I had no idea that helping three women start up their home-based sugaring salons would catapult my career in a new direction.

Even though there are now a handful of sugaring salons in Chilliwack, Just Peachy is still known in the community as THE place to go for sugaring! We have the largest number of staff, are open the most days, and have the longest hours. But it's not just our long hours and weekend availability that puts us on top – it's because Just Peachy is the industry leader. I pioneered the hair removal path in the community by educating thousands of clients annually, speaking at women's events, and being in leadership roles. It's my face people remember and my van that people honk and wave at when they recognize the logo and branding from our years of advertising. Just Peachy was the first of its kind, and our years of experience and education have kept us in the top spot in terms of business recognition and client retention. We have more than a few certificates and awards hanging on our walls, and I am very proud of the reputation we've created. I worked hard to get the business to where it is, and I take pride in the fact that every single client leaves happy after having another positive experience in my establishment.

Before the shutdowns, I'd been too busy to even consider exploring any other direction for my business. On top of everything I did at the salon, I held many volunteer positions in the community including teaching the afterschool theatre program at Chilliwack Middle School and serving on the board of directors for a number of local and international organizations. Now, I had nothing but time on my hands. If there was ever a time to pivot my business, this was it! And it didn't take long for that lightbulb to click on above my head. I started thinking about how I could not only improve my personal financial situation, but also grow the Just Peachy brand while helping countless women in my community and across the province. So many women had lost their jobs due to the pandemic and were now at home with their children, unable to afford daycare and needing to work from home, or were desperately seeking a career change. If I had time to teach, I was sure there were hundreds of women out there who had time to learn. Everyone was used to Zoom calls now thanks to Covid, and the majority of businesses who were succeeding and thriving during this unsure and unprecedented time had all moved online. Why couldn't I? And just like that, the Just Peachy Training Academy was born.

As I began to put my lessons together, I started to see a pattern throughout my working life. Before becoming an entrepreneur, I had taken the Sales and Marketing Certificate Program at the University of the Fraser Valley and then worked in both the sales and marketing industries. One of my favourite jobs was being the ad controller at the Abbotsford Times newspaper in my twenties, where I played Tetris with the ads in order to leave the correct amount of space for editorial. I also worked as the social media coordinator for several companies, for which my skills as an ad controller very much came in handy. The career I had just before having my children was as the marketing coordinator for a large computer software company, where I created magazine advertisements and launched marketing programs for thousands of clients across North America. In addition, I created playbills for local theatre companies, programs for churches, and designed graphics for hundreds of businesses, events, and organizations. Although I had never previously made the connection between all of the random jobs I'd had since I was a teenager – including being a commercial photographer, retail sales clerk, MC, wedding planner, writer, librarian, career counsellor, food blogger, bank teller, theatre instructor, administration assistant, web designer, and more – I could now see the glaringly obvious connection: all of the skills I had learned in these many different positions contributed to me working as a trainer in a very creative manner. This was my passion! I had been training myself to do this for the last two decades, I just didn't know it until now.

However, getting over twenty years of knowledge out of my brain and into both video and text format was a huge job! This was the biggest project I had ever undertaken in my life. Every day, as I would walk my dog in a three-kilometre loop around my home, I would grab my phone and dictate notes – everything from sugaring terminology to social media tricks, government mandates, and bookkeeping pointers. Documenting everything I could think of, organizing it into a step-by-step instruction manual, and trying to create visually appealing bite-size chunks of information became my new job. As I would be dictating notes about something I learned in university, a memory would pop up about a business idea, tip, or trick that my parents, both entrepreneurs themselves, taught me when I was a child. Every day I would spend hours working on this new project, creating a template for success that was proven through my years of experience both owning my sugaring salon as well as coaching others to be successful in their own businesses. I wrote from both of the perspectives I knew: a scared newbie just starting out and a successful community leader with years of experience under her belt. I had already done the steps and lived this life, I just needed to put what I had learned into a format that would show everyone it was possible for them to also become a huge success.

Today, as I sit here writing the first draft of my chapter in this book, I am starting a new chapter in my life as well. The Just Peachy Training Academy has two training dates per month set out for the rest of the year, and already we are more than 50% sold. I have had to hire two new people to help the salon keep running smoothly as I hit the road and travel across BC, offering hands-on training in both sugaring and business support. The online community I have created in the last few months will help everyone who takes my training continue learning as they grow their business day by day. Within moments of launching my online business support program, I had two friends reach out to hire me as their new business coach, saying that they had always looked up to me as a businesswoman and industry leader.

I haven't stopped smiling once over the last few months, and the perma-grin on my face isn't going away anytime soon. The next level of my business will be a game changer for everyone involved, and I can now clearly see how to get there one amazing step at a time! I am so excited to be the number one cheerleader for every woman who feels alone, stuck, or unsupported, and I cannot wait to take them from a hopeful idea to the grand opening of their new business venture. If I could pivot my mindset and my business, anyone can! With or without my help, no one needs to feel small in their lives or their business. Nobody should feel like a side character in their own story.

"The year that shall not be named" was challenging in so many ways, and yet I am also grateful for it. Shifting my mindset in a time where I could have very easily given into frustration and depression has given me the best gift ever: the ability to discover and work on my passion every single day! I hope that my story is able to inspire others to finally grab the bull by the horns and take the necessary steps to pivot both their mindset and their business so they can become the best versions of themselves.

About Amy Andersen

Amy Andersen is a writer, sought-after speaker, and leadership facilitator as well as the owner/founder of the Just Peachy Sugaring Salon. What began as an opportunity to design the business that would work for her family catapulted her drive and passion for being able to help others do the same. In addition to still seeing clients two days a week, Amy now focuses on growing both her businesses and has surrounded herself with a team who all believe in collaboration over competition.

During the shutdowns in 2020, Amy expanded her business by creating the Just Peachy Training Academy, which guides women through the process of creating their own sugaring salon. She has also begun working as a business start-up coach, helping women across Canada who are looking to start over in their careers or find a way to work from home while caring for their small children. With her step-by-step plan and proven template for success, she can help anyone pivot their mindset and be successful in business.

Amy lives in Chilliwack, BC with her two teenage boys and her Aussiedoodle, Aurora. In her free time she enjoys propagating house plants, reading mystery novels, and planning road trips.

www.justpeachysalon.ca

4

Conquering Fear through Surrender

By Lisa Chan

"You must give up the life that's planned in order to have the life that's waiting for you."
Joseph Campbell

Conquering Fear through Surrender

By Lisa Chan

By all accounts, I have led a successful life. My CV lists a fourth marriage to the same man that has lasted twenty-eight years, with two awesome kids who love each other to death; an MBA in entrepreneurial management from UBC; a successful real estate development business; a company named TrufElle (truffles for HER) with the mission of using cannabis-infused aphrodisiac chocolate and self-disclosure to inspire women to be sexually liberated; and a commitment to help others reach their potential in every way possible.

In the early days, though, I was known as a control freak. I attended to every little detail in both my personal life and my professional one. And I assumed that total control, together with a simple method I developed for getting what I want, was the key to my success. As you will see, I was only half right. The method has three steps:

1. Discover what you want.
2. Ask for what you want.
3. Get what you want.

Simple, right? Not so fast. There is a stumbling block built into the method that I had not anticipated, but which I came to see as crucial to the entire process.

Discovering is simple enough. Before you can be ready to ask for something, you need to have a clear vision of what it is you want. Let's say you want to start a new business. Your clear vision begins with two areas of inquiry. The first is around your business. What kind of business do you want, and what do you want it to do? The second is an inquiry about yourself. What are you really passionate about? Will your business reflect your passion? This is perhaps the most important aspect of Discovering. Creating and developing a business is hard work; it takes a lot of time and there will be many obstacles. Only your unwavering passion will pull you through this tedious process.

The first thing to note here is that Discovering leads almost immediately to Asking. However, asking for information is much different from asking for someone's involvement, compliance, or money. This is where the rubber meets the road! Asking risks rejection, and rejection hurts. It is woven into the human psyche from a very early age, when Mommy or Daddy said no to our heartfelt requests for something or were too busy to hear us. Soon enough, we interpret rejection as a comment on who we are. It lays bare our inadequacies, our flaws, the scars on our sense of self. This is deep stuff, so it is important to come to terms with it. Once you know what rejection – and the fear that accompanies it – are all about, you can begin to see your way through it. And getting through it changes the stumbling block into a breakthrough, a triumph of will.

Two breakthroughs occurred in my life that cemented the importance of walking through the fear no matter what the anticipated results might be. One was a personal epiphany after embarking on what I thought was an extremely risky venture, and the other was seeing my daughter take her own path through her fear of rejection.

The first breakthrough began when I woke up one morning and realized that my personal life had become a monotonous routine that stretched on into the future, without a single hill or curve to add a little mystery or intrigue. The problem was that after twenty-four years of being married to a great man, our sex lives were, in a word, boring. And in that moment, I discovered that boring sex was not really sex at all. So, I resolved to take responsibility for it. If I wasn't getting what I wanted, it was because I had not asked for it.

Making that decision brought up all those fears and anxieties. Ask for what I wanted? In *sex*? Yikes! What if my husband didn't respond the way I hoped for? What if he looked at me with a quizzical look that said, "That's really weird"? Or, what if he winced in an expression of distaste? What if he ran from the bedroom screaming, "She's a witch!" It could affect our lives forever after; it might even destroy our sex lives completely. These were the disastrous scenarios I envisioned.

However, once I understood the problem, the options were clear: I could stay safe and sexually unfulfilled, divorce my husband in the hope of finding someone more sexually compatible, or take the risk of asking for what I wanted and actually get it. These are, in essence, the same options we have in business. Not asking for what you want has the advantage of certainty, but then you don't move forward. Asking and being rejected also produces certainty (if a disappointing one), but now you are free to move on to the next possibility.

Clarifying my problem also stimulated something else: a lustful nagging curiosity that I knew would never end if I decided to stay safe. My path was clear; all I had to do now was summon up the courage. So, I opened a bottle of Amarone, poured two glasses, took a deep breath, and began the inevitable conversation. I asked for what I wanted and those ooey gooey feelings welled up inside me as my husband listened, smiled, and said it was all a wonderful idea! I was elated beyond anything I had ever experienced. The knot of fear, anxiety, and anticipated negative self-evaluation simply dissolved. Since that day, our sex life has been an earth-shattering, bone-rattling, soul-screaming adventure.

The breakthrough with my daughter requires some history. During a family vacation in China, my daughter Cadence, fourteen months young, suffered an extraordinary accident in a marketplace. A man tripped and fell against a boiling pot of water, spilling its contents all over her as she sat in her stroller. When my husband and I arrived at the hospital, Cadence was in the ICU. The attending physician told us that she had burns on fifty percent of her body, and that she might not survive the ordeal – babies with her level of injury have only a ten percent survival rate. I collapsed inside for a moment, but then I simply refused to believe it. "Doctor," I said with as firm a voice as I could muster, "I know my daughter will make it. She's a very strong girl and never gives up. She will pull through. Now let's skip the bullshit and talk about the recovery stage." In my head, I was thinking, *It's just a burn; how can my daughter possibly lose her life from a burn?!*

Fortunately, Cadence was a fighter and she pulled through

– nevertheless, my sweet little girl required a lifetime of regular surgeries. As the young body grows and stretches, scars don't. Instead, they constrict, endangering locomotion, blood circulation, and bone growth. In order to prevent or reduce these complications, they used surgical procedures such as cutting, stitching, and skin grafting. Pain is a constant companion for Cadence, and the scars, though somewhat diminished over time, will never really go away.

Eventually, the day I had been dreading arrived. After her swimming lesson, Cadence stood in her UV bathing suit and watched another girl taking a shower. When I prodded her to take off her suit, she huddled in a corner of the room and said she was embarrassed because she was "different." Her head was bowed, and she had the saddest face. I tilted her face up toward mine and told her she didn't need to feel embarrassed because she was beautiful. "What really matters, sweetie, is the beauty inside us." Cadence didn't seem convinced, so I held her close until a little smile appeared on her face.

In retrospect, what I said was disingenuous. The "beauty inside us" is a platitude, a social device to compensate for physical abnormalities. The real issue was how Cadence felt in her world, and I should have zeroed in on that. I should have empathized with her feelings and told her that I completely understood. This was another lesson in control. Whenever I saw how others looked at her scars, I would act as though their stares didn't exist. I thought that taking a stoical stance would impress Cadence more than the onlookers, but of course she would have noticed the dissonance. I knew I couldn't control what others would think or say about her scars as she grew into a young woman, and it gnawed at me continuously. I even encouraged her to cover them up to avoid the issue entirely. But I also knew I had to let go of the urge to protect her from a cruel world. I had to let her find her own way. My job now was to nurture her self-confidence, self-empowerment, and, yes, some self-defence. So, I applied the 3-Step Cycle to see if it would lead to a giant Get for both Cadence and I.

It was immediately clear to me that the big Get here was Cadence being able to move past all her resistance to showing her scars in public – in other words, to arrive at a state of mind that was free of all her fear of exposing her *imputed* flaws. I say "imputed" because a scar is unarguably a scar, but is it really a flaw? Or is it merely a unique characteristic?

One way to achieve this is having Cadence show her scars to everyone she met until her resistance simply melted away. But I asked myself if there was a bolder solution where she could safely tell the whole world in one courageous act. And then it came to me: a TEDx talk!

When I told my daughter about my outrageous plan, she was immediately excited. We sat down at the kitchen table and worked on a script, honing it to her liking over the course of several weeks. She practiced and practiced until she had it down pat.

Finally, the day arrived. Cadence was standing on stage in a short sleeve dress, displaying the relics of her accident and subsequent surgeries for the entire world to see. She talked about her ordeal and the struggle to walk through her fears of rejection fluidly and confidently with a certain luminescent aura about her, free of it all. And she talked about her journey of overcoming people's judgments of her with simple, unconditional kindness. So proud I was to witness this spectacle that tears welled up inside me and I felt a whole new dimension of love for her.

The takeaway is simple: if Cadence can do it, anyone can. Whatever you are up against, either in business or your personal life, think for a while about that vulnerable young woman on stage baring her scars and her soul with confidence. Her talk was not simply a performance; it represented a profound transformation of her inner being.

This was the point in time when I became convinced of the power of the 3-Step Cycle and realized that it could be applied in any area. Furthermore, I realized that what I called its "stumbling block" – the fear that comes up in the asking step – is the cycle's most important feature.

Control is a defence mechanism. In order to avoid disappointment, rejection, and failure, we control every little detail in our life and keep a tight rein on our emotions and our vulnerabilities – our scars! However, in the deeper personal realm, what we miss out on are the opportunities that comes to us on the other side.

First of all, walking through the fear builds courage. Once you see that the worst-case scenarios are really not so bad, you will experience a certain exhilaration and greater willingness to either ask again or ask someone else. That's the second thing: in both business and your personal life, you are now that much closer to a favourable result. In fact, some sales manuals advise that yes only comes after twenty or more noes. As sales strategist, speaker, and author Jill Konrath observed, "To be successful, it's critical to tackle your fears. If you don't, they become major obstacles that limit you." Loosening up, becoming more spontaneous, and walking through the fear of rejection are options the soul favours.

I have seen these benefits in my own life. Towards the end of one of our trips, Cadence said to me, "Mommy, I like you more when you're on vacation." When I asked her why, she said it was because the mommy at home was always on the phone or the computer and didn't really listen to her. The mommy on vacation was more patient and more attentive. It broke my heart to hear this, but at the same time, I had to admit that she was right. She made me realize that I did like myself more when I was on vacation. Less committed to controlling things, I had more time for what was more important: enjoying my sweet daughter's company.

The wonderful thing about human beings is we adapt. Cadence's accident demonstrated to me that no matter how much I think I can control things, there's a limit, and it's a lot closer than I think. This life requires a modicum of surrender to the way things are, and I have learned that it's about finding the sweet spot between total control and total surrender.

All of these lessons were put to the test when I started my business, TrufElle. I knew what I wanted to achieve (or Get), so the Discovering step was relatively short. My idea was to create a safe environment where women and couples could explore their inner desires and talk about them freely. Talking about sex in public is almost a social taboo; certainly, talking about personal preferences, especially the more "eccentric" ones, brings up resistance and could easily make others uncomfortable. That's where the cannabis-infused TrufElle chocolates come in. I knew from my own experiences with cannabis that in appropriate doses, it produces euphoric feelings and makes everyone more congenial and willing to open up to each other. I also knew that cannabis enhances both the sensations and the communication in the sex itself.

To move forward, I merely had to ask people if they might be interested. I began by asking several women in relatively long-term relationships (six years on average) when they last had sex. They couldn't remember! This convinced me that women needed a safe setting to talk about their sex lives and normalize the expression of their unmet sexual needs, ideally with their partners present. I began to see that love and sex are skills to be learned, and that the learning begins with open communication. These conversations are much easier when mellowed out on cannabis, in the right setting, and with an experienced facilitator. After exposing my own intimate desires to my husband and reaping the rewards, I was in a first-hand position to guide other women in the process of getting to yes in sexual adventuring.

The Getting in my plan also proved to be relatively easy. Several women were immediately interested and soon brought their partners with them. The chocolates were a big hit, needless to say. Everyone became warm and more intimate with each other, and I asked appropriate questions to steer the conversations to the heart of the matter. Very soon, we embarked on a free-wheeling sensuous discussion of our sexual desires, our feelings, and how we can live more authentically. Inhibitions dropped away and souls were bared to one another. Couples became closer and were eager to take the intimacy home with them.

TrufElle has since moved on to host educational workshops and weekend retreats that teach the seductive art of provocative conversations, massage, and flirting. It's all about creating a greater priority and intention around sensuality. After each event, the women who attended are more sexually heightened and their partners are delighted to see their wives' sexuality come alive again.

I can't tell you how fulfilling TrufElle is in my life. The connection with other people on this level is exhilarating, profound, and heart-warming. There's juice here! I formulated a plan, asked the right questions, and bingo! I've also personally benefitted from the interactions I have with my customers, many of whom have become friends. It's important for women to have quality time with girlfriends as it fills their cup up with love, which in turn makes us better when we go home to our families. I am definitely a more patient mom and compassionate wife because of our amazing TrufElle parties.

No matter how you decide to use the 3-Step Cycle, once you have completed the Asking step the Getting is relatively easy. By that point you will have conquered your fears, you will be less controlling, and you will have become much more spontaneous. Your passion will be written on your face. Furthermore, you will find that the people you interact with on your professional and personal paths through life will be much more empathetic, more willing to hear you and attend to your most intimate needs.

I intentionally used the word "cycle" to indicate that it is a never-ending process. Once you complete one cycle, apply the three steps to something more adventurous. Learn how to master French kissing on Youtube, ask someone to join you, and then practice constantly. Ask your partner how to create more passion in your relationship on a daily basis. Build your personal brand on social media – research how to set it up, ask the right people to help you, and create engaging content. Create a web page and consider writing regular blogs. The 3-Step Cycle's applications are endless!

Excited? You should be! This is the beginning of a whole new you. So get out there and Discover, Ask, and Get your way to everything your heart desires.

About Lisa Chan

Lisa is the founder of TrufElle, a company on a mission to enlighten cannabis curious women to be liberated in their sexuality. She met her husband while still in high school, and after twenty-eight years she became well aware that she had to find ways to keep the passion alive in her marriage. Her drive and curiosity led her to experiment with cannabis, herbs, and chocolates as aphrodisiacs. The confection, in combination with Lisa's guided explorations, opens hearts and minds to uninhibited spontaneity.

Lisa's newfound awakened journey at age forty led her to re-discover her sensual desires. Through the creation of TrufElle, she is able to share the education and tools she has found to re-ignite that feeling of intensity and intimacy for people who are in love.

Lisa holds an MBA in Entrepreneurial Management from the Sauder School of Business at UBC. As a serial entrepreneur, she owns established businesses in the field of real estate development and property management. She is passionate about inspiring young girls and women to own their worth and live their best life NOW!

www.trufelle.com
Email: desiretrufelle@gmail.com
Facebook: TrufElle
Instagram: @desiretrufelle or @lisa.chan.vancouver

5

Out of the Shadows

By Marlies White

"There is no failure except in no longer trying."
Elbert Hubbard

Out of the Shadows

By Marlies White

The world is constantly changing, a fact I have come to know as being undeniably true over the seventy-three years of my life. Sometimes, change is for the better; sometimes, not so much. Often, what makes the difference is stepping into our power and living our passions.

I was born in Germany in 1948, just after the second world war, and came to Canada at six years old not knowing any English – it was like being reborn and having to learn everything all over again. Once I learned the language, though, life was normal by Canadian standards.

As I grew up, I dreamed of perhaps becoming a movie star, a neurosurgeon, or even a writer. However, family finances were tight, so my career options were limited by what my parents could afford to help me with. I became a hairdresser for a few years, then switched over to working as a teller in a major bank. Over the next twenty-five years, I rose through the ranks to become a loans, mortgage, and investment advisor and lender. I then retired from the banking world in 1994, though I continued to work by helping my husband in his medical practice.

Then, in 1997, we lost my brother-in-law to prostate cancer. I did not know it at the time, but this unfortunate loss would change my life in ways I never could have imagined. It inspired the creation of a product that can forever change how a person lives and ages – a product that has been my passion for the past twenty-two years.

Reeling from the pain of losing someone so close to us in the prime of his life, my husband and I began to seriously think about how we could keep our loved ones healthy well into their golden years – essentially, how we could help them stay young as old as possible. This passion led to the creation of Kelowna's best-kept secret: our patented Youth Formula, created in 1998 by my late husband, Dr. Philip A. White.

Philip was an innovator who I believe was far ahead of his time. He had been Chief of Staff at Kelowna General Hospital for seventeen years as well as serving on the boards of various cancer agencies. He also ran a full medical office as a much-loved family practitioner in Rutland, BC, and his patient's love and respect for him is still evident to this day. He was passionate about helping people live the longest and healthiest lives they could. He always said it was easier to prevent an illness than to fix it, and that made him the perfect person to take on the enormous task of formulating a product which some say is a Fountain of Youth.

So, what is this secret behind this incredible formula? As we age, our levels of Human Growth Hormone (HGH) decline. In fact, research has proven that as early as age twenty-five, our pituitary gland begins to slow the release of HGH. By the time we turn sixty, our pituitary is only releasing about one third of what it did in our twenties. Evidence points to these diminishing HGH levels as being directly related to many of the ways aging ravages our body. Therefore, by restoring our HGH levels to what we had when we were younger, we can help slow, stop, and in some cases even reverse many aspects of the aging process as we know it today.

There are two ways to elevate growth hormone levels. One is through HGH injections, which is both expensive and potentially dangerous if not extensively monitored. The other is through a secretagogue or growth hormone releaser that encourages the body to release more of its own HGH. This is what Youth Formula does. It is completely safe and natural, working in harmony with our bodies' own processes.

To get our product out into the world, Philip and I created our company, SomaLife, outside of his medical practice. I was passionate about being the one to bring this business to life. The company had a humble beginning in the basement of our home, with me using my banking knowledge and organizational skills to get us up and running to the best of my ability. But as we tried to grow the business and find success, we faced many obstacles. Making our way through these challenges took vision, commitment, hope, and a desire to help others live a longer, healthier life. It took being focused and working tirelessly to build an infrastructure to support this product we ultimately wanted everyone to benefit from. Failure has never been an option, and in the end our efforts paid off. We are now an international company, yet we still treat our customers like family – some have even been with us since the early days.

As we put our Youth Formula out into the world, we

quickly began to receive feedback from our customers about how their lives had changed. They told us how they had more energy, were sleeping better, had lost weight, and just generally had better health. I was, and still am, so proud and overjoyed to be a part of helping so many people better their lives.

Between 2002-2004, we decided to work on expanding our customer base. SomaLife was an anti-aging company from the beginning, and we knew that to have the biggest impact, we needed to open its market to younger adults. With that, we applied to the National Sanitary Foundation and the World Anti-Doping Association – two organizations that test professional athletes for supplements that will affect their performance – and were able to get a certification that recognized Youth Formula as being safe for pro-athletes to take. We were then able to introduce our Youth Formula under a new NSF-certified label with a product we called gHP Sport. Today, many of the major league baseball players are taking gHP Sport to supplement their strength and conditioning, which gives them a winning edge.

Even with these amazing products under our belt, getting SomaLife established was quite the challenge. Despite his brilliance, Philip did have his flaws. He repeatedly hired people who did not have proper managerial qualities, and their management styles made it obvious that they did not share my vision of helping people – that they each had their own agenda. One of the management staff even went so far as to tell his friends that SomaLife would provide them with access to houses, planes, and luxurious travel. It was about what they could get, not what they could give. These unqualified managers nearly sank the company on many occasions over the years, yet I always managed to bail it out using my own personal resources.

For over twenty years, SomaLife ran a bit like the movie *Groundhog Day*. In this film, Bill Murray lives the same day over and over again; that was us. We would hire a manager, see him lose money as he did not market the product or the company, do a personal bail out, fire the manager, hire a new one, and on and on. Quite often our customer's orders had to be put on backorder as these managers had not ordered inventory with enough lead time to meet the demand. This is how you lose customers!

The most soul-destroying thing in all of this was that soon after Philip and I married, I learned that he had been unfaithful throughout our time together and had no intention of stopping. I thought about leaving, but since I was the one keeping SomaLife afloat, doing so would have caused the company to fold. I was not willing to let that happen. I had put so much time, effort, and love into this company, and I truly believed in the product. The only thing I could do was suck it up and just keep being present. I kept showing up at the office, many times with a heavy heart, as I fought to save both my marriage and the company.

Interestingly, while I was supposed to be the face of SomaLife, I was always sidelined and kept away from the running of it. I never felt heard, either by my husband or by any of the managers – who, by the way, were all men.

Sadly, Philip passed away of pancreatic cancer in 2015, which came as a shock to all who knew him. Despite the conflicts we'd had within our relationship, I still mourned the loss of such a brilliant man who had worked so hard to change the world. Now it was completely up to me to keep SomaLife going, and the challenges were not over yet.

You know how someone can get on your very last nerve? Well, that happened to me with our latest manager, to whom

Philip had given ownership of the company shortly before his passing. It was done through a share swap where no money was exchanged – we only received new shares in the manager's US company. Philip's decision was based on all the pie-in-the-sky promises this guy made. He kept telling Philip he was creating these fabulous marketing pieces that would blow up sales and bring in new customers, yet he was never able to show results. What was also frustrating is that he could never produce current financials, so we did not know where we stood. He was extremely charismatic but had absolutely no substance. This individual had coerced Philip into giving away MY company. Philip was a brilliant doctor, but as a businessman, not so much!

That last nerve I referred to earlier came in the form of this manager asking me for personal money to help him float his lifestyle – not the necessities or business expenses, but fun extras that were not my responsibility. If history repeated itself, it would be a loan that he would never pay back. I'd had enough! After spending years dealing with an unfaithful husband and a never-ending stream of so-called "executive office managers" who did nothing for the company, I was done with letting other people take advantage of me. It was time to seek legal advice. I was advised that my best option was to put the company into receivership, which would allow me to dissolve and then rebuild it. SomaLife owed me a great deal of money at this time, and I lost a good portion of it by placing the company into receivership, but I had two of the most amazing lawyers guide me through the process so I would be able to buy the company back.

Before I pulled the trigger, I called all the company's creditors and explained what I was about to do. I then either paid them in full or offered a settlement to make sure everyone at least got something. I hated having to offer settlements as I have always honoured any debt I had, and I grew up learning to avoid having debts in the first place – my own fiscal responsibility is what made this all possible. I am thankful that I had a lot of support from all those who were owed money by the company.

Once I dispatched all the bad karma, I could focus on rebuilding what had once been a company with great potential to help others improve the quality of their health. I did not want to let down all the people who had come to depend on our supplements. This was perhaps the scariest thing I have ever done. To save my vision and my dream, I had to jump into the deep end and pray I could swim. There were a lot of moving parts involved in dissolving one company and transferring all the various accounts to the new one. There were suppliers to contact and all the utilities to be switched over, as well as all the technology that drove the business. After two years, I was finally able to close all the old accounts and operate completely under the new management: ME!

SomaLife was now running very lean, with minimal expenses. The staff was happily down to just two of us: Kim, who does the shipping and customer service, and me, who negotiates with suppliers, pays the bills, and manages the financial end of things. I did not really know much about marketing, so I hired a media company to post to all my social media accounts and work with me on website development. I also re-established the monthly newsletter we used to print back in the early 2000's, which the media company uploads to our website each month. This newsletter has one page that provides information on health and a second where we post testimonials and share any specials we may be offering. I find it to be a fun way to keep in touch with our customers, and I love writing the content each month.

Things were just beginning to settle down when we were hit by the COVID-19 pandemic in early 2020. This was a devastating time for a lot of companies, and many had to close their doors. For us, it was merely a hiccup in the grand scheme of things. By now we had become very resilient, and we had already set ourselves up to work from home a year prior. We were working smarter by not having all the trappings of a brick-and-mortar business. We had found that almost 100% of our sales were online, so we put our resources into marketing; even though we are now in the third wave of Covid, our sales are flourishing. Our expenses had been brought down as low as possible, and we have been able to pass those savings on to our customers to help them through this difficult time. Our many satisfied customers and our world-class, one-of-a-kind products have almost made us bulletproof, and all the work I have put in since taking over the company has paid off.

Making the hard decision to fight back and step out of the shadows has also led me to pursue something I love to do almost as much as running SomaLife. Remember when I told you I wanted to be a movie star, neurosurgeon, or writer? Well, I did not become a movie star or learn to do brain surgery, but I have begun writing. I started with baby steps, contributing chapters to the sixth and seventh WOW books. I wrote about aging with moxie and thriving through turbulent times, having experienced both scenarios. I then went on to write a full book on my own, which launched February 3, 2021. *Because He Could* achieved #1 bestseller status in the "Love and Loss" category on Amazon, as well as reaching the top ten in two other categories.

Since Philip died in 2015, I have finally come out of the shadows in more ways that one. Everything I have done to further the company and share the story of achieving good health through supportive supplements has led me down a road that now gives me a great deal of joy. SomaLife has always been my baby, and my mandate is to make sure that Philip's legacy continues to shine brilliantly – though seeing as I am the one who has kept the dream alive, perhaps it is as much my legacy as his. Becoming a writer has opened a whole new world to me, and I have learned to forgive those who have wronged me. Maybe what I have lived through is not what I would have chosen for myself, but it has made me into a strong woman who has beaten the odds and succeeded. If you have a dream, DO NOT give up on it, EVER!

Oddly enough, through everything that happened, I never felt like a victim. I was merely biding my time to come out of the shadows. Where there is truth and honesty, there will always be light.

About Marlies White

Marlies White, in 1998, was inspired to start her business, SomaLife, in response to the loss of a close relative. Working with her late husband, Dr. Philip White M.D., the pair created a series of products directed at promoting better health for others. SomaLife is an Okanagan-based health, wellness, sports nutrition, and age management company that develops, manufactures, and markets its proprietary line of one-of-a-kind products locally, nationally, and internationally.

Now with over two decades of experience under her belt, Marlies leads her company to grow with the vision of changing more lives with natural health and wellness products, including a Pet supplement specifically created because of her love of animals. Marlies lives by her personal motto of "you do what needs to be done, helping as many people as possible along the journey." Marlies looks forward to fulfilling her husband's legacy, and hers, in the coming years.

In February 2021, Marlies achieved Amazon #1 Best Seller status for her own book, *Because He Could*.

www.somalife.com • mewe.com/i/marlieswhite
www.theisfp.com/members-2/marliessomalife-com/
Facebook: Marlies White • **Instagram:** @whitemarlies
LinkedIn: Marlies White • **Twitter:** @Marlies_White

6

Never Give Up

By Olivia Repnicki

"If you don't love yourself, there is no love to give."
Olivia Repnicki

Never Give Up

By Olivia Repnicki

Finding my purpose on this earth has been quite a journey. There were many times when life tried to knock me down and I had to find ways to keep my feet as firmly on the ground as I possibly could. It has not been easy, but the future I can now see in front of me is proof that it is worth it to keep going.

As a young girl, I remember wondering what was wrong with me. I could feel other people's emotions very deeply, and for a very long time I didn't understand why. I felt like I was different from everyone else – almost like I was from a different world.

Growing up in Eastern Europe in the 1980s, life was challenging. The spiritual world, aside from religious beliefs, was not well understood or received. As a little girl, my maternal grandmother was the only person I could find comfort in – the only one who understood me. Today, I know that she was also spiritually gifted. She saw the gift in me and tried to explain it to me as best as she could, although there was only so much I could understand at such a young age. She also tried to guide and encourage me to explore my feelings and intuitions.

In the mid-1980s, my parents emigrated from Eastern Europe to Canada in hopes of finding a better life, mostly due to political reasons. Unfortunately, this meant I was separated from my grandma, and she died shortly after. I was devastated. It was now me against the world, still trying to understand why I felt so much. I often tried to escape these feelings through music; when I danced, I felt like I was floating above the earth in my own little world.

As a teenager, I tried hard to tune out these deep feelings, and I often felt lost and misunderstood. I did not believe I had a lot of support from my parents as they didn't understand me, so instead I sought that support in all the wrong places – even getting in some typical teenage trouble. Sometimes I felt happy; other times, I was quite confused. School was not my strength, probably because I was struggling to figure out my life purpose, and I did not always do what was expected of me.

My journey as a young adult was not easy either. However, I always tried to have fun, look for the next adventure, and live in the moment in an attempt to figure out who I was. Looking back, this would explain why I got into relationships that might not have been the best for me. However, each one has helped me learn more about who I am and envision what I want my life to look like. I also explored various career options – some were quite successful and fulfilling, yet I always felt like I was missing something.

One day, I met a man who introduced me to Reiki. He explained how powerful it is for helping others, and more importantly, how it could help me find my own purpose. I was intrigued, but I was not ready to accept my gift yet. It was still a pivotal moment for me, though, as learning about Reiki reminded me of the strong emotions and intuition I have always had within me. Slowly, all these feelings I had been afraid to explore began to reappear in my life. It took me quite a few years, as well as some travelling in search of my own self, to realize that I am gifted. Some people are really good at math, languages, writing, or singing; I am good at understanding others' feelings and determining their purpose. I started remembering what Grandma used to say to me about trusting my intuition, and about feeling like I had a sixth sense. I now understand that this gift was passed on to me by my ancestors.

When I searched deep inside me for a sense of inner peace, joy, and happiness, I started to better understand my gift. The power of my empathy and intuition opened my heart, and then it started to empower my life.

In 2012, I gave birth to my beautiful daughter who I know is also gifted, even more so that I am. Motherhood seemed to amplify my own spiritual gift, which became extremely strong. I could not fight these feelings any longer; I knew I needed to open that door. I decided to take a Reiki course a few years ago, but unfortunately it did not work out at first. I struggled to find a Master who I felt was right for me. I did not feel attuned, and I did not feel ready. After a year had passed, I decided to try again. This time I found an amazing woman who also became my mentor in so many aspects of my life.

I began this healing journey at the toughest point in my life. I was still learning how to be a mom and was in a difficult relationship. I was also facing family challenges and was now changing careers. But perhaps this journey came to me exactly when I needed it most.

Upon completing the course, I was so excited and eager to start helping people and sharing my beautiful gifts. However, I knew I had to heal myself first. I started the twenty-one-day Reiki cleanse to help me move forward, make a commitment to myself, and empower my own being through Reiki attunement. As I went through this process, my physical and emotional pain as well as all my fears began to come to the surface. I had extreme, painful physical symptoms as my body worked to cleanse itself from the inside out. As time progressed, I became more aware of my strong beliefs in healing and positive attitude. I was hopeful and prepared to face all that was yet to come. I made a commitment to take care of my body, to get stronger emotionally in order for my body to become my intuitive receptor, and to release the energy needed to heal. I started to ask for inner guidance, and I trusted the process of healing.

This was the beginning of my journey to self-discovery, which continues to this day. The key in my journey has been finding ways to ground myself, reconnecting with my inner peace, and trusting my intuition to lead me to my purpose. I work on taking small steps towards the person I want to become, which creates opportunity for big changes.

In 2018, I shifted my focus from healing myself to helping others heal. I began to share this beautiful Reiki energy with the world by creating crystal bracelets. I have always believed in the power of crystals – I see them as talismans that can help us through life's obstacles and challenges. We are often drawn to certain ones without understanding why, but when we touch them and close our eyes, we can feel their energy. It is pure magic! Crystal Obsessions was born from my passion, my intuitive gift, and my desire to help others. Each stone carries a unique positive quality that, when matched with the person wearing it, creates jewelry with a healing purpose.

When I was first starting out, I invested all my savings into purchasing the best quality crystals and began creating jewelry in my bedroom while my little girl was asleep. I created lines of bracelets for protection, prosperity, anxiety, and so much more. Once I gathered enough inventory, I went out and searched for places to distribute them. Thankfully, when you believe in something so much and put your entire heart and soul into it, your passion will shine through and your tribe will find you. I soon met a woman who opened the doors of her business to me, and then more opportunities started to flow. People become drawn to my jewelry as if the energy within these pieces spoke directly to their soul. Then, people started contacting me to have custom jewelry created just for them, and this was the turning point for Crystal Obsessions. Imagine having jewelry made of precious stones that were carefully selected in order to help you set your life on a positive path and push away any struggles!

The process of creating these custom pieces is so beautiful. The client and I have a one-on-one session where I can look deep into their eyes, read their soul, and help them understand everything that is happening to them and why. My intuition guides me to select the crystals that will most benefit their needs at this time.

One of my first clients, who has become an amazing friend, persuaded me to start performing Reiki as well instead of just hiding behind the crystals. She became my first client and still receives treatments to this day. I set up my guest room to perform Reiki sessions and people started to come – and then they just kept coming. Apparently, the news of my beautiful healing jewelry and Reiki powers spread fast. It seemed like overnight, I had so many clients that I couldn't take any new ones.

Reiki is like a massage for your soul, and when you find that one trusted Reiki Master who is the perfect fit for you, the experience is unbelievable. It helps achieve clarity, peace of mind, relaxation, and healing of past and present trauma. In each session, I help my clients relax and go into a meditative state. I then guide them into the light and help them find a path to their full potential on this earth, provided they have the necessary willingness, openness, and readiness to receive this practice. And the more Reiki I performed, the stronger my abilities became. I started to communicate more deeply with the other world. The spirits of loved ones started to come in with important messages, helping me to heal those who needed healing.

One of the most touching stories to date is of a man whose wife had recently passed. He was devastated, and he came into his Reiki session looking for peace. When I began the session, I immediately felt his wife's spirit hugging his aura in a very loving way. In my mind, I asked if she would like to join, but she did not want to. Towards the end of the session, she showed me some rose petals she was holding between her fingers, then she went to his ear and whispered, "Thank you." After the session, I told my client what I saw and felt, and he started to cry. His words were, "You are amazing." Once he composed himself, he told me that prior to coming to see me, he had cut a few of her favourite roses from the bush in front of their house and placed them in a vase in the living room. Stories like these are so precious; each and every session is magical.

With time, I became so strong in my mediumship that I decided to invest more time and money into educating myself as a medium. And with my business growing rapidly, I decided to transform my basement into a Reiki haven. Once again, I invested all I had into making this the best experience for my clients. The room came out beautifully – it was an oasis of calmness! In this amazing space, clients come and sit with me surrounded by candles, crystals, and soft healing music that speaks to their soul. The room allows my clients the freedom to speak their feelings and come to peace with themselves. My goal is always to create a magical, healing place for everyone who comes to me. At this time, all my clients came to me through recommendations from someone I was already seeing. I didn't don't advertise my services anywhere; I strongly believe those who need me will find me.

However, not long after I created my new Reiki haven, COVID-19 arrived and everything changed in the blink of an eye. The pandemic hit me hard, both personally and professionally. I had to close the doors of my business, and my relationship with my partner was also on the verge of ending. So many hardships in such a short period of time. I did not want to go into hiding, though, as I was afraid of my own hurt and pain. I needed to stay on a positive path; I needed to have a purpose. I had a little girl who was counting on me to keep going. She did not understand what a pandemic is, why everything was changing, why mommy and daddy were arguing, or why she could not go outside and play. I had to be strong for my little girl, for my clients, and most importantly, for myself.

I started reaching out to my clients to make sure everyone was okay, and this led me to offer distance Reiki to everyone who needed or wanted it, even if they couldn't afford it. I knew that people needed my services now more than ever. I also performed long Reiki sessions on myself in order to cut off all the energy that no longer served me. I needed clarity and a calm mind in order to be the best I could be for all those who matter to me. Self-care was so crucial during this uncertain time; if I was not well, nothing else would work. I kept reminding myself that it was okay to let my emotions run wild sometimes, and that it was okay to cry – I tried not to cry around my daughter, though, because I knew that I could gain strength from her.

I needed to pivot, again. I was a soon-to-be single mom with a business that had to close its doors and no possibility of finding a job in the middle of this pandemic. There was nowhere to run, nowhere to hide. I began evaluating my next steps, and I decided it was time to go back to the basics. I focused on learning how to use social media to generate more business, and once I put this into practice, my distance Reiki, readings, and custom jewelry began picking up. People were contacting me from all over the globe about my crystal bracelets; my energy and my encouraging posts spoke to so many.

Once I made a conscious decision to turn away from what wasn't working and focus on what I know, what I have control over, and what I need, everything started to fall in place. I learned so much about my business and the endless possibilities that come from serving others, marketing through social media, and selling products through word of mouth. And with this learning has come a new passion. In today's busy world, where fear and lack of confidence play a big role in preventing people from achieving their dreams, I want to help people – especially women – discover their strength and potential. I want to help them gain the clarity and courage they need to move forward. I want to guide others through their healing journey to find happiness, increase their confidence, and learn to turn whatever life throws at them into opportunities and endless possibilities. Most importantly, I want to help women learn how to love, respect, and believe in themselves.

Despite all the challenges I have faced, I have turned my dream into a success story. For those of you who are reading this, my message to you is to never give up, believe in yourself, seek your purpose, and always aim for your dreams.

About Olivia Repnicki

Olivia is a passionate, intuitive, self-renewed, intriguing woman who, through her long journey of self-discovery, found a unique talent that can help others in their own path. Her spiritual gift and her passion for crystals inspired her to learn about Reiki and begin creating crystal bracelets imbued with healing powers. Soon she expanded to offering Reiki sessions out of her home, first in her guest room and then in a custom-built Reiki haven.

Today, Olivia is both a certified Reiki Master and a medium. She is an intuitive healer with a passion for guiding you through your life journey so that you can reach your full potential. In her sessions, she uses Reiki universal energy as well as her gift of mediumship and her strong intuition as an empath to help her clients become stronger and healthier.

www.crystalobsessions.com
Facebook: Crystal Obsessions by Olivia
Instagram: @crystalobsessionsbyolivia
Email: olivia@crystalobsessions.com

7

Living Unapologetically

By Michelle Berezan

*"Spread love everywhere you go.
Let no one ever come to you
without leaving happier."*
Mother Teresa

Living Unapologetically

By Michelle Berezan

No one could have ever predicted what happened in 2020. While this was a year of hardships for many, for some of us it was the year we changed our lives forever. Personally, the shutdowns that came with the COVID-19 pandemic put me on a path to realizing my greatest passion. I didn't recognize at the time that it was only the first step on my journey – that pursuing my passions would give me tools that I would not only use to help others, but also to help myself.

When the world first shut down, I realized how isolated and depressive my life had become in the years leading up to this event. I called my doctor and shared the sadness and isolation I was experiencing, and he promptly prescribed me a low-dose antidepressant. For the first time in a very long time, I felt relief – I no longer had to endure this unnecessary and overwhelming sadness. And once I didn't feel like I was slowly sinking in quicksand, I was able to realize my passion to help as many people as possible.

Over the next three months, I wrote an entire course, entitled Peace Power Passion, and sold it to my first ten customers. Thus, MB Brands was officially created! The goal of this course is to help people change their life physically, spiritually, and emotionally as well as to help them monetize their passions. The first session took ten brave women through my six-week extended course in three short weeks – things were going to be opening up at the end of that month, so we needed to get the course finished before some of the participants headed back to work. Their honest feedback provided me with valuable information to improve the course even more. They all told me the same thing: this course had an abundance of information that definitely needed to be spread out over six to twelve weeks. They were also all pleasantly surprised that they were able to learn valuable skills they could immediately apply to their lives.

However, just as my new company was starting to take off, the seasonal summer resort I was manager at decided to re-open. The timing was less than desirable, but I felt compelled to honour my commitment there. I then worked every single day for three months straight with limited help and no childcare. My previous anger and frustration quickly returned, and by the end of those three months, fighting with my kids had become a daily occurrence. I knew I needed to reconnect with my children, but I also just needed a break. I was miserable, and it wasn't fair to any of us for me to continue on like this.

Then, I had a realization. Since I was in need of some physical, spiritual, and emotional improvement, why not take my own course? Obviously, the course was created based on many of my own personal experiences and the tools I had learned along my own journey, as well as those of my clients. That being said, I could see how quickly I kept getting off track from my life's purpose every summer, when my work hours were extremely extended and my stress level was magnified – not to mention the added frustration of the pandemic. I needed to re-apply my knowledge as a student. What is described next is my journey both from my experiences leading up to creating my course and from the past six months.

First up was module one: identifying my obstacles and finding solutions. My obstacles were quite easy for me to name: my inner dialogue was sending me down a negative spiral, I had become disconnected from my children, my house was in disarray and full of clutter, I was feeling completely isolated, and I had lost my connection to my Higher Power. As for solutions, well, I was already working on them by taking my course!

My inner dialogue was top priority as it would be the key to improving all other aspects of my life. Thankfully, this was addressed in module two: defining what having compassion for myself looks like and beginning to put that into action. My course covers a multitude of ways to achieve this, but for the sake of brevity, this is what worked best for me. To get started, I went back to basics and came up with three positive statements about myself: "I am a good mother," "I forgive myself for my mistakes," and "I am beautiful." I wrote these statements on my bathroom mirror and read them out loud every time I entered that room. Next, I needed to open up the dialogue with my Higher Power; for me, that involved prayer, mindful meditation, and chanting. I began implementing regular mindful meditations and Buddhist chanting to help quiet my inner chatter. Praying became an ongoing task for me – I felt so lonely at the time that I needed to connect throughout the day.

Another huge component in having compassion for myself was connecting with my children and repairing the damage that had been done to our relationships. We reimplemented our family prayer together every night after family reading time. This was a special time for me to hear my children pray and learn what and who they prayed for. My boys still pray for homeless people every night, and it melts my heart every single time. Also, just the act of sitting on my bed in a circle and holding hands with each other is a superior bonding moment. I also reimplemented a "no screen time" policy from Sunday at 5:00 p.m. to Friday at 6:00 p.m. Now, I do not judge the screen time you give your kids - I myself have had weeks where my kids have had an abundance of screen time. However, I felt that at this time, this was the best approach for our family to reconnect. We are also about to start a 30-day family challenge of absolutely no screen time as I am writing this chapter (you are welcome to email me to find out how that went). The point is to find what works for you and your family and forget about what anyone else thinks.

This is a quick synopsis of the beginning of my path to finding compassion for myself. I will not explain everything I did here – it was a lot! I share the rest of this journey in my full-length book, as well as in my Peace Power Passion course.

As I continued to work on changing my inner dialogue, I moved onto the next module, which deals with personal values and setting boundaries. During this module, I examined a list I had made of my personal core values – a comprehensive explanation of our family code of conduct and my personal boundaries as they pertain to my core values. These were all still at the forefront for the vision I had for myself and my family. Our family code of conduct was then posted in our kitchen so my children could also start to learn how to become what I refer to as "the five C's": confident, capable, committed, compassionate contributors. I decided to change my current focus to not only becoming a successful educator, but also experiencing and raising incredible children. Along with my writing, my counselling, my coaching, and my course, I desperately wanted to contribute four phenomenal people to the world.

Module four addressed decluttering my physical, emotional, and spiritual spaces. When I first started decluttering my physical space, I hired a feng shui expert to come through my home and offer suggestions. I then spent the following three weeks implementing his suggestions and clearing out all unnecessary belongings, which resulted in approximately thirty percent of what we owned. However, this has been an ongoing journey—within three or four months, my house had returned to its original cluttered state! Once I found myself retaking my course, I discovered that it was time to get re-energized. I spent a weekend watching tiny house shows and minimalistic living vlogs, and this gave me the motivation I needed to start again. The one common statement made by most people on these videos was that if they had known what they know now back when they first started moving towards minimalism, they would have just spent two weeks getting rid of everything right away. They all said they didn't miss anything, that cleaning their home was now quick and easy, and that they had less anxiety and stress. They also said they created systems to ensure the clutter never comes back. I also re-read my own module on decluttering as well as all my research materials from writing my course. Every piece of material I could find had the same message: get rid of your excess "stuff" and quit spending money on things you don't actually need.

At this point, I realized I had been buying stuff just for the sake of spending money – most of what I had bought over the years was non-essential. I bought stuff, then bought stuff to store the stuff in. It was a vicious cycle. So, I went into each room and started packing up the non-essentials. I applied the 90% rule: rate each item on a scale of one to ten, and if it is below a nine, get rid of it. Also, when you're not sure about something, use the 20 rule: if you can replace it for less than twenty dollars in less than twenty minutes, then get rid of it. I then created my own rule: if you can't pack up your house in a day, you have too much stuff! Today, I use the approach of making sure I can pack up each room in an hour or less – that being said, I am a fast packer. This has allowed me to live a decluttered life rather than a minimalistic life.

The rewards have been substantial. I am extremely proud to say that I have donated or sold approximately sixty percent of our household belongings. I now live a life with so much less stress and anxiety, and it is an incredible feeling. One benefit I did not expect, though, was that I would have so much more free time after making this change. I'm not spending so much time cleaning and putting things away. My children can now easily see where everything goes, and this means they can help Mommy keep the house in order. My relationship with my kids has been rehabilitated and blossomed into one filled with kindness, compassion, and love. I no longer yell at my kids because I no longer feel like I am doing everything with no help. We all enjoy our family time.

Next, I decluttered my emotional space. I kept my calendar light and analyzed who I was spending my time with most. I quickly discovered that I had one toxic friendship, so I stepped back from that relationship. I now no longer allow myself to stay in situations that are mentally or emotionally negative, and I no longer accept being dismissed. Next, I decided to focus on expanding my base of good friendships. I put more effort into connecting with the people I cherish and paid attention to any new people I met so I could get to know them and possibly cultivate some new friendships – so long as I felt they would be a positive influence in my life. I have also learned how to live my life completely unapologetically. I no longer feel the need to justify my life or parenting choices to family and friends. I feel grounded and confident in my choices without listening to the background noise of unsolicited comments.

Finally, I decluttered my spiritual space. I created a special space in the house where I could go for my quiet time, and my kids have learned not to interrupt me while I am in there. However, they are more than welcome to join me, or to use this space for themselves whenever they need to. It is quite an accomplishment to train two three-year-olds, a five-year-old, and a seven-year-old to all let mommy have uninterrupted time in her quiet space, but my amazing children have honoured my connection with my spirituality and have shown interest in developing their own. This has melted my heart in ways I cannot even describe. Staying connected spiritually so that I can hear and trust my intuition has been a huge piece of my journey, and I want to share that with as many women as I can.

Next on my path was module five, where I determined what I wanted my life's impact to be. I created a personal vision for myself as well as personal, professional, and life goals. The more in-depth I went, the more focused I became. The clarity I had after this was irreplaceable. As I mentioned earlier, my kids became a huge focus for me during this process and were intertwined with many of my goals. The deeper love and more powerful connection I have with my children today has filled my heart with a fullness I didn't think I would ever achieve. This all made it fantastically evident what I am passionate about: raising four phenomenal children, as well as teaching other women how to achieve the amazing inner peace and joy I have had the privilege of accomplishing in my own life.

By the time I reached my final module, how to monetize my passions, figuring out my path to achieve this was easy. I now had the clarity I was missing before, and with clarity comes great joy and inner peace. Carving out my own path for my life has been an interesting journey so far, and I am excited about the next chapter in my life.

This course has taught me the value in applying my own skill sets to my life on an ongoing basis. I now have more time, more energy, and more clarity to focus on my passions. I am preparing to do world-schooling with my children in a few months and could not be more excited. I have opened myself up to new friendships that have been amazing. And not only am I happier, but my children are also happier too.

I have since shared my own experiences and taught my course to many more women, who have shared their success stories with me: getting the raise they didn't think they deserved or were too afraid to ask for, reconnecting with their spouse, leaving a toxic relationship, going back to school to study what they're truly passionate about, the list goes on and on. I've been told by women who have had previous trouble expressing themselves that they have now found their voice and can be more assertive in asking for what they need. The best feedback I received was being told, "Not a day goes by where I don't apply at least one aspect of what I learned in your course!" This warms my heart and reaffirms what I have chosen to teach. Knowing that I have helped other women find their joy in life is humbling, and I want to continue to share this with as many people as I can.

Too many women have either lost their jobs during Covid, are unhappy with where they are at, or are struggling to move forward with their career, personal life, or spirituality. Through my Peace Power Passion course, I coach women on how to create the lifestyle they desire. We first address their inner challenges, then declutter their lives to create the path for their desired changes, and finally teach them how to monetize their passions. For so many women, this is all possible from the comfort of their own home, which will ensure long-term security. I can attest to how effective and powerful my course is because I have spent the past six months applying it to myself and my own life. My previous students check in with me from time to time to report how amazing their lives have become and what changes they made because they took my course. I love what I do, and I love being a mom to my four incredible children.

Women have a voice and deserve to be heard. Once you learn to ignore the outside chatter (other people's opinions and suggestions), to quiet the inside chatter (your inner dialogue), and to forget societal rules (everything you've been taught since you were a child), you can create and follow your own path. This is what I refer to as living unapologetically. My chosen career path is to support women in finding their inner voice and inner power to positively and passionately propel them forward in their lives. Once we all learn to unapologetically live our lives in a way that brings us happiness, fulfillment, and connection, we will make the whole world a better place.

www.MichelleBerezan.com
Email: admin@michelleberezan.com
Facebook: Michelle Berezan • **Instagram:** @Michelle_Berezan
Twitter: @MichelleBerezan • **LinkedIn:** Michelle Berezan

About Michelle Berezan

Michelle Berezan is a teacher. She is a teacher of kindness and compassion to her four beautiful children. She is a teacher to people suffering from addictions as a certified addictions counsellor. She is a teacher to people experiencing perinatal/postpartum depression, disordered eating, stress, and anxiety as a registered clinical counsellor. She is a teacher to the masses as a best-selling author and creator of the Peace Power Passion course, in which she helps individuals break through their mental blocks and discover a more joyous way of living. She also uses her experience as a mother of high-spirited children and multiples to pass on firsthand knowledge of how to overcome stressful parenting situations and build a strong family unit. All of this makes her the ultimate student in her life.

Michelle has spoken at residential dependency treatment centres about her own journey of overcoming addiction as well as on improving one's own life condition through personal accountability and giving back. Along with other charitable endeavours, Michelle makes it a priority to be of service both locally and abroad through her foundation SWAG (Service Work Around the Globe). She continues to speak out about improving your life after experiencing addiction, depression, and motherhood in her latest book, which you can expect to see on shelves shortly.

8

From Powerless to Powerful

By Lily Zhao

*"Owning our story and loving
ourselves through that process is the
bravest thing that we'll ever do."*
Brené Brown

From Powerless to Powerful

By Lily Zhao

What words come to your mind when you think of femininity? Pink, soft, flowery, light? In today's society, femininity is often perceived as weakness, and many women have become overly masculine in an effort to conform and adapt to what is seen as more valuable in the world of business. However, the contrast I observed between the lives of masculine women and feminine women opened my eyes to what is truly powerful. I finally took a path that is authentic to my core and became exactly who I was meant to be, and this was only possible due to the self-love I developed through overcoming the many challenges I have faced.

I disliked myself as a child and adolescent, due in no small part to the many traumatic events that occurred during my early years. Growing up in Japan, I experienced racism from quite a young age. As the only Chinese kid in my kindergarten class, I was alienated by my classmates, which made me feel like there was something wrong with me. As a result, I always needed to prove to myself that I could fit in. As the years went on, I tried harder, pushed harder, no matter what. I started to use negative self-talk to motivate myself, and it worked – that is, until I had a mental breakdown. Several, in fact – one in elementary school and one in high school.

My peers were not the only ones who had an impact on my self-esteem. In Japan at the time, conforming to society was seen as being very important. As a result, I was brutally beaten by my kindergarten teacher for expressing myself. I remember that day vividly. I was playing in the playground one minute, and then the next I was in a room with my teacher. She stripped my clothes away and started abusing me physically. I couldn't figure out what I did wrong. From that day on, I lived in fear. I was desperate to feel safe and to avoid being hurt again, so I learned to tame myself. This led to silencing my own voice. I thought that my opinion didn't matter, and even if it did, I was too afraid to speak up. I felt like I was worthless. So, I put on my mask and learned to be fake – inauthentic, but pleasing to the people around me.

Then, in high school, an event occurred that put me over the edge. I was raped by two of my guy friends whom I trusted, and it was extremely painful. I did not know how to deal with the trauma, so it manifested in a destructive way. I couldn't respect myself or my body. I HATED myself, and I tried to numb that pain with anything I could find – alcohol, drugs, sex, just anything. I had zero self-respect or self-worth. My self-esteem was so low it felt like it was in the negatives. I was disgusted every time I looked at my reflection in the mirror.

I am also a recovering people pleaser. When I had low

self-esteem, I couldn't say no to others due to a fear of being disliked or disappointing others – being liked was more important than valuing and honouring my inner voice. I used to say yes to requests I wanted to say no to because I was afraid of being rejected. As I participated in this negative cycle of not meaning what I said and did, I stopped trusting myself, and then I lost respect for myself.

Due to a lack of self-worth, self-respect, and faith in who I was and how much of a difference I could make, I spent many years living in fear, doubt, and depression. I hid behind masks and false personas because it made me feel safe. I struggled with self-confidence, self-doubt, and imposter syndrome. But inside this suffering was a seed of change. Once I realized how much I was suffering, I knew that something had to change – it was too painful to live this way for rest of my life.

As I examined the source of these insecurities, I realized that all of them stemmed from lack of self-love. In order to silence my inner critic and crush my goals, I began to practice self-love by learning to value myself – and this saved my life.

Self-love can be defined as caring for yourself through emotional connection and being loyal to yourself. It goes hand-in-hand with self-esteem, which is based on how we value ourselves. Self-love comes before self-esteem, and both of them together boost self-confidence.

The true cost of self-doubt is high. When we doubt ourselves, we risk never seeing anything to completion and being left feeling unfulfilled. For example, I had always wanted to write a book, so one day I finally decided to work towards that goal. However, I wasn't sure about my own writing, so I threw it away. Continuously abandoning myself and my work led me to believe that I was not worthy of anything in life. Self-doubt prevents us from pursuing our dreams – in fact, doubt kills more dreams than failure ever will. Thankfully, it doesn't have to be this way.

For me, the turning point came from a conversation I had with my soul sister, Lisa. I asked her if she ever doubted herself, and she answered, "Why would I?" This moment was powerful. After all, she was right. Why *would* we doubt ourselves? From then on, every time I had to make a decision and that little voice of doubt crept in, I was able to battle it by repeating this mantra: "Why would I doubt myself? I believe in me."

I also recently read a book by Glennon Doyle called *Untamed: Stop Pleasing, Start Living*, and when I was done, I felt a new level of liberation. This book taught me that when we stop pleasing others, we are free to please ourselves. I began to imagine what my life would look like if I just focused on pleasing myself, and this created a powerful shift. I started living an authentic life, and this created space for my friends and family to live for themselves.

In order to shift from powerless to powerful, I knew that I needed to cultivate healthy self-esteem, self-confidence, and self-love. So, I looked back into my childhood to see who I was before I was forced to conform to societal norms. And once I did, I could see that I was born with an energetic, creative, playful, curious spirit. I was born to be the light and sunshine for others, freely moving and dancing my way through life. With this knowledge, and with my new practice of self-love, I have been able to explore activities and passions that I previously would have cast aside. As I am writing this chapter, I am also taking my first art class. I have always loved art, but I never gave myself the chance to pursue it until today. It has been so liberating to choose what I truly love instead of what others expect of me.

Self-love allowed me to discover who I authentically am

and created the possibility for me to design a life where my core, soul, and heart are aligned. It stopped me from worrying about what other people think and helped me stay true to my authentic self. I believe I am a human cat with an inner unicorn personality who has been put on this earth to help women find their feminine core, live their life authentically, and make a positive social impact. And even though I get many confused facial expressions or judgments when I share this, I choose to stay in my lane of life. When I doubt myself, I harness my inner unicorn to push through the cloud of fear and doubt into my vision and goals. With an abundance of self-love, I am able to make firm, clear decisions rooted in a strong sense of self-acceptance and self-knowledge.

Practicing self-love also gave me the courage to speak my truth and believe that what I have to say is valuable and important. I learned to say what I mean and mean what I say. And as I became less concerned about what others think, I also became freer to make career choices that were in alignment with what I wanted in life and how I wanted to make an impact in this world. Public speaking was once one of my biggest fears, but self-love gave me the courage to face my fear and speak on TEDx about the danger of people pleasing. Self-love also gave me the inspiration to create a podcast to interview the unicorns in the world on how they were able to stay true to themselves and design their dream life.

Self-love can benefit your career in many ways. For one, you are open to taking more risks because they feel less risky. Part of practicing self-love is seeing your worth as being something you define rather than something that is defined by people or circumstances. When we know our intrinsic value and separate our worth from the potential outcomes, there is less damage if things don't work out the way we intended them to. This is very freeing because it shifts how you approach your life and the choices you make.

You will also experience less burnout or work-related illnesses because you learn to put your own needs first. Many of us find ourselves consistently putting work ahead of our needs, and while it may be an occasional necessity, doing this on a regular basis can lead to career burnout. This also has an impact on the quality of our work – when my body starts breaking down, I become less focused and less productive. When I put myself first by working out every day, eating nutritious food, and meditating, I feel sharper and more energized. From that state, it is much easier to tackle any obstacles that come my way.

Yes, self-love has many, many benefits – but it is not the end of the story. I recently discovered something that changed my life forever, and that is the power of stepping into my authentic feminine self.

Femininity is a lost art, and I want to share with you how this art form can powerfully transform your life. To demonstrate this concept, I will walk you through the real lives of an overly masculine woman (MW) and a feminine woman (FW) that I have known and observed.

Let me introduce you to MW Mandy. She is in her masculine all the time as she perceives femininity as weak. At home, she emasculates her man and does not allow him to do anything for her as she believes that will hinder her independence. She does everything on her own, and so she is exhausted and burned out – yet she still refuses to ask for help. Her man does not feel like a man around her and is constantly walking on eggshells, afraid of being criticized by her. He feels restricted and controlled. Neither of them are truly happy in this relationship. Many businesswomen who are climbing the social and professional ladder, like Mandy, disconnect from their feminine core due to the perception that it is less valuable.

On the other hand, FW Felicia allows her man to be a man and taps into her feminine self to create polarity of masculine and feminine energy. She understands that being in her feminine allows her man to feel strong, powerful, and useful. She immediately praises him every time he does something right and shows him appreciation and respect. She allows him to help her, and he is happy that he can serve her in this way. He feels like a winner in her presence, and both parties are fulfilled and happy in this relationship.

Interestingly, this is no different than relationships we have in the workplace. How often have you seen females in your workplace abusing the dark side of the masculine as power? They will yell at people and try to make other women/men feel inferior, all because she feels like she needs to prove herself in the workplace. She comes home exhausted, burned out, and not quite sure why she feels out of alignment with herself.

On the flip side, there is a feminine version of this woman. She may be a CEO, but she unconditionally embraces her femininity as she lets everyone feel like they are helpful, needed, and strong. You don't need to force your power onto the people around you. A woman whose success comes from the depth of her feminine spirit communicates radiance, and a businesswoman who has understood that her radiance is what magnifies her success becomes unstoppable.

This contrast helped me realize that instead of pretending to be a man and doing everything from masculine energy, I could follow the feminine path. Instead of focusing on the masculine way of "doing," I could focus on the feminine way of "being." This is another act of self-love that helps me stay true to myself.

It may sound counterintuitive to focus on being instead of taking action, but once I made this switch, my goals and dreams manifested at the speed of light. As I sat in my gratitude for what I already had, I started to attract more amazing things into my life. For example, I wanted to write a book this year, and then my dear soul sister Denise told me about this amazing opportunity to write in the WOW book series. When I focus on being joyful and believing that something wonderful is about to happen from moment to moment, it naturally manifests into my reality.

Being a feminine woman is choosing to honour the gift offered at birth from that core essence of femininity. It is being in flow with the present moment, fluid and open to life's challenges, unbridled and nurturing of beauty and relationships. It will change how you relate to both men and women and improve the quality of your intimate relationships. When you are in your feminine essence, life is magnified through your heart and soul. Your feminine energy allows you to connect with yourself, trust yourself, and love yourself. For example, when I tap into my feminine core, I am in tune with my intuition. And when I am connected to myself and listening to my inner voice, I make better decisions in life.

While connecting with your feminine energy is vital, we should not completely discount the masculine. In December 2019, I attended Tony Robbin's signature seminar "Date with Destiny," in which he shared his profound knowledge of masculine and feminine energies. He also shared that when we learn to cultivate both energies, we become magnetic. Masculine energy is active, logical, powerful, and focused; feminine energy is fluid, graceful, elegant, sensual, and gentle. When we counterbalance our masculine and feminine energies perfectly, our conscious energy is tempered by our intuition and emotional intelligence. This increases our unique presence, which then improves our influence.

Knowing the power of femininity, how do we tap into it? There are several practical steps you can take. The first is to **make creativity a part of your life**. The feminine is the creative force – it created me, you, and the whole universe. Embracing it involves more flow, more fun, more play, more gentleness, more creativity, and more collaboration.

Another step you can take is **spending time with feminine women**. As the saying goes, we are the average of the people we hang out with. So, if you want to be successful, surround yourself with successful people. If you want to connect with your feminine core, surround yourself with women who already have. I usually go to a high tea or do something with my girlfriends while wearing a flowy, feminine dress.

The last step I will share here is to **stop living in your head and get into your heart**. One quote from Tony Robbins' seminar will stick with me for life: "If you are in your head, you are dead. Get into your heart." When we are in our masculine energy, we are analyzing, strategizing, executing, pursuing – we are living in our head, and there is a place for that. If we want to feel alive, though, we have to come down to our heart and feel. To reconnect with your feminine energy, indulge your senses. Taste the decadent foods you love. Go shopping and feel all of the soft fabrics. Enjoy a beautiful environment such as a café shop, a beautiful hotel, or a spa. I love smelling scented soap in the morning, seeing fresh flowers when I wake up, and listening to classical music while reading.

When you dare to live authentically, life responds in kind. So, step into the fullness of who you are, put aside your disempowering behaviours, rediscover who you truly are at your core, and practice self-love. When we embrace who we are as a woman and understand our intrinsic value, we realize that we don't need anything other than our own truth to be and have anything.

And that, dear reader, is power.

About Lily Zhao

Lily Zhao is an investor, TEDx speaker, and certified life coach. She became an investor at the age of twenty, which created the financial freedom she needed to work on her life calling. Prior to pursuing her passion in helping women find self-love and emotional freedom, she studied health sciences at Simon Fraser University to understand health and wellness at a holistic level. Her experiences of trauma and the challenges she faced in her life gave her the drive to help women heal, love, and accept themselves unconditionally.

Today, Lily is a femininity embodiment coach with a passion for helping women tap into their feminine core and discover their true superpower. She is also currently working on creating a podcast to interview other unicorns in this world who are living their dream lives, allowing them to share and pass down knowledge and wisdom that will empower women for generations to come.

www.coffeewithunicorns.com
Email: lily@coffeewithunicorns.com
Instagram and Facebook: @lilyzhaoxx

9

Embracing a Changing World

By Moira Cohn

*"Accept, then act. Whatever the present moment
contains, accept it as if you had chosen it.
Always work with it, not against it ... This will
miraculously transform your whole life."*

Eckhart Tolle

Embracing a Changing World

By Moira Cohn

I've always loved a good makeover. Influenced by rags-to-riches fairy tales, throughout my childhood in South Africa I dreamed of a tall, dark, handsome prince who would one day whisk me away and make me happy. We would live in a "castle" in a safe, affluent neighbourhood and have two kids, a cat, and a dog.

I was lucky enough to meet my prince during my last year of high school, and we dated for six years before getting married. Ninke was born nine months after I decided to sell my day spa as we planned to immigrate from South Africa to Vancouver, British Columbia. We welcomed Chloe into our family two years later, and the four of us paved the path for other family members to join us in Canada.

After nine years in our new country, I purchased my second

spa. It was so much fun updating and renovating the business and then seeing the revenue double in the first year. I told you, I LOVE makeovers! However, at the two-year mark my gut prompted me to sell. I handed the keys over to the new owner on August 1, 2008, and a month later the recession hit Vancouver. Over the years I've learned to trust that uneasy feeling in my gut, even when my accountant and others advise otherwise.

I enjoyed working for the new owner and supporting her with the day-to-day operations of the spa. I was feeling relieved and deeply content with my full life. That is, until one day I light-heartedly asked my husband if he still loved me, and the answer was no.

In that moment, my world came crashing down.

It is said the truth shall set you free, and I have found that to be the case. Although the truth emotionally flooded me like a crushing wave at first, it also made me realize I was no longer the woman my spouse married. It was an opportunity to have authentic conversations as we navigated new waters, perhaps for the first time. It also made me ponder, who am I? Once I had become a wife, mother, and business owner, I lost myself in these roles as they were defined by society. Can you relate?

Wondering who I was opened an opportunity to study image consulting with Karen Brunger at the International Image Institute in Toronto. Image consulting addresses improving your image through appearance, behaviour, and communication, and it was incredible. Aside from discovering my signature colours and unique style, I also learned something truly mind-blowing: thoughts become things. We are always creating our circumstances, but it's only when we consciously create that we feel fulfilled.

When I arrived back from Toronto, a series of events

completely changed the trajectory of my life. I came home to a husband who was frustrated with his job and ready to move on, and he had been called to interview at a different company. I saw this as the perfect opportunity to apply my newfound knowledge. "Great," I said, "how much would you like to earn annually?" He looked at me cautiously and gave me a number. I then told him we were going to go shopping for a navy suit that cost one percent of what he wanted to make. Clarence resisted at first, hesitant to spend that much money on one outfit, but I told him I would just charge it to my credit card. This was before I worked on my own money mindset; I'll share more about that later.

The following week we went to Harry Rosen in Vancouver and purchased a gorgeous Cavalli suit that hung on his tall frame like it was made just for him. He looked stunningly handsome and professional.

Clarence went to the much-awaited interview and came back with an offer. I asked him what it was, eager to know if this manifesting thing worked – although deep down, I was sure that it had. Strange, even though I'd never tried this experiment before, I knew there was truth to it. So, when my husband told me the offer was less than what we both wanted, I simply said, "That's the wrong offer."

Tired of putting out fires at work, Clarence decided to accept the job offer anyways and handed in his letter of resignation. Eager to keep their valued employee, the company counter-offered and things went back and forth for a while. I vividly remember Clarence arriving home with eyes as big as saucers. "They gave me everything I wanted. They made me VP of technical operations and gave me a forty-five percent raise." I quietly stared at him for a while, then exclaimed, "That's my suit!"

When I reflected on all this a few months later, I realized it all came down to energy – you feel different when you are dressed to impress. In order to get what you desire, you have to put yourself in the same energetic vibration.

After seeing the success of my husband's suit, I finally understood how all this worked. For something to manifest, two things are necessary: surrender and clarity. Clarence surrendered to the fact that he was leaving and thus detached from his job. Not wanting him to leave, the company made him an offer. He turned it down twice before they finally asked, "What DO you want?" It wasn't until he was clear about what he wanted that it actually showed up.

Sometimes, though, figuring out exactly what you want can be a challenge. A few months after returning from Toronto, I was offered a position at Langara College in Vancouver teaching a personal development class among other image consulting courses. I remember asking the students to write down what they wanted and seeing them all stare off into space, pen and paper in hand. One day, I decided to try something different. I asked them to write down everything that annoyed or frustrated them. Holy smokes! Heads went down and pens started scribbling; there was an eagerness to get it all down. I then asked the students to write the opposite of what was just noted in order to reframe their thoughts. There was one caveat: they had to refrain from using "not" in their sentences. What each student ended up with was a clear list of personal desires. It was powerful!

Of course, deciding what you want is just the first step. Have you ever gotten clear on your goals only to get tripped up by the gap between where you are now and where you want to be? Me too! It's debilitating – or at least it was. Then I realized I don't have to figure out the how, I just need to align myself vibrationally with what I would like to achieve. It's like living on the fourth floor of a high rise while my deepest desires reside in the penthouse suite. Everything I want already exists; I just need to vibrationally align with it. This is what I help my clients do: I show them how to attune their vibrational energy with where they want to be by changing their mindset and image.

Excited to transform women's lives, I started seeing private clients around the same time I accepted the teaching position. I eagerly met with Trudy, my first paying client, for a colour analysis. I draped her with this pale blue fabric, which made her beautiful blue eyes pop. "Trudy," I said, "look how amazing your eyes are!" I'll never forget her reply: "Moira, I always wanted brown eyes."

This stopped me in my tracks. How could someone with such beautiful eyes want something different? And also, how could I showcase my client's unique features if she didn't accept and embrace them? In that moment, I realized that what holds many of us back is not our looks, status, education, or resources, but rather the inability to see and embrace our true selves. If I was going to help women transform, I would have to go deeper and explore the origin of their self-doubt and self-worth.

I have found that when you are open and ready, the right book, mentor, or program reveals itself. So, a few years later I found myself enrolled in counselling courses at Clearmind International. It has been a journey of profound self-love as I ventured to discover my family of origin and the main sources of my subconscious limiting beliefs. I realized that not only do the clothes I wear send messages both to myself and the world around me, but also that unless my beliefs align with what I desire, my dreams will always be just that: dreams.

No one can experience shift and change on this scale

without it impacting your immediate family. My eldest daughter described this situation beautifully. When a couple gets married, it's like two people getting into a rowboat together. With oars in hand, they row in unison, moving strongly towards their dreams. Sometimes, though, the dream fades for one and they stop rowing, making it harder for the other. Then, that person has a different dream all together and starts rowing towards that instead. The boat stays in one place, driven in opposite directions, unable to achieve forward motion again until one of the people has the courage to get out of the boat and into a different one. This is what happened to Clarence and I; we hugged goodbye and started to row our own boats.

The girls were in their late teens when we separated, and for the sake of ease I moved out to live in a nearby high rise. I had never lived by myself – one of many firsts that would follow. It was thrilling and exhilarating, until the elephant in the room made itself known. I've always been diligent about paying bills but avoiding looking at my money. Financially forced to move into a smaller shared space, I found myself sitting on my bed and crying, not knowing how I was going to make the minimum payments on my $50,000 credit card debt with the income from my part-time job. Lesson learned: not paying attention to money results in poverty.

I felt such deep shame and kept my debt a secret for as long as I could. It wasn't until I became a counselling student that I realized my avoidance of money was birthed when I would see my dad stomping around the house like a bear with a sore foot, complaining about the family budget. In my child's mind, I figured that avoiding all things money would keep me from the angst my dad was displaying. This is how limiting beliefs are birthed.

The thing about hitting rock bottom is you can only go up

– but only if you do something differently. As the saying goes, "insanity is doing the same thing over and over again expecting different results." So, instead of avoiding, I leaned in. I enrolled into a year-long online course about healing my money story and managing my finances, started the Smart Women Finish Rich book club, and took an investment course. It wasn't until I went through this healing process that money started to flow into my life via a stable, well-paying job; a settlement from the divorce; and gains on my stocks in my self-directed investment account.

Two years into a stable position as a building supervisor, I remember looking at all the gorgeous photos of places I wanted to visit in Europe and thinking about how great it would be to actually experience them. Then there was a knock on my office door, and when my employer entered I heard myself saying, "I would like to take a month off and travel Europe." There is truly something magical about knowing what you want and leaning into it.

Travelling is so beneficial to the mind, body, and soul. When we experience new places and people, it gives rise to wonderment, curiosity, and expansion. Dormant parts of yourself wake up, and a desire to live life to the fullest wells up within you. Now I can hear you saying, "Uh, hello, Covid!" And to that I say, you don't have to go far to see these benefits! Consider exploring a new neighbourhood, province, or state. Simply changing your environment naturally makes you curious, and this is a wonderful state to let life in.

Coming back from this eye-opening trip to an office job with regular hours felt discombobulating. I had the resources to start my third business, and I felt drawn to do so. The only thing I needed was time. So, on Feb 27, 2020, I quit my job and enrolled in Tony Robbins and Dean Graziosi's Knowledge

Broker Blueprint program to start my online mindset coaching and image consulting business. Two weeks later, the world shutdown due to the COVID-19 pandemic.

There is a big difference between choosing change and being forced to change. When we are faced with such an incredible obstacle – one that we cannot get rid of, and instead must go through – there is one thing that will allow us to adapt, and that is ACCEPTANCE.

A past experience in Ninke's bedroom taught me the profound impact of acceptance. One day, Ninke invited me to come watch music videos in her bedroom. She thrives on being organized and tidy, unlike her sister, so it came as a bit of a shock when I stood in her doorway and saw clothes on the floor and an unmade bed. Normally I would resist entering the abyss of a teenager's messy bedroom, but since Ninke was usually tidy I decided to make myself comfortable on her bed. Once I got settled beside her, I had a clear view of her open closet. I was surprised to see that in contrast to the heap of fabric on the floor, the clothes in her closet were hung and organized by size and her shoes were neatly paired. I said, "Ninke! Your closet is so tidy and organized!" She smiled and responded, "No mum, my ROOM is!"

My eyes started to drift to her desk in the far right corner of her room, where her notebooks were neatly stacked. On the opposite side of her desk, there were three bookshelves with her books organized by author. How was it possible for a room to be both tidy and messy at the same?

This experience taught me the importance of perception. From the doorway, I could see the floor and bed but not the closet, desk, or bookshelves. Once I made myself comfortable on her bed, I had a different view. The one thing that allowed me to view her room from a different perspective was

ACCEPTANCE. Standing in the doorway, I had one of two choices: I could resist the state of her room and turn away, or I could accept it and enter. I realize this was also true of life itself. Both good and bad exist simultaneously; my experience depended on whether I choose to accept or resist.

Our world is ever changing, and our survival relies on our ability to adapt and innovate. As I'm writing this chapter, a year has passed since the world shut down and I am amazed at some of the innovations that have come out of it. Pizza ovens are being repurposed to produce face shields for frontline workers, stay-at-home moms are selling face masks on Instagram, and seventy-three-year-old grannies like my mom are attending church services on Zoom. All around the globe, people are accepting the challenges placed before them and adapting in order to both survive and thrive.

So, how did I adapt? Image consulting and abundance coaching simply didn't feel relevant with all the challenges people were facing, so I was spiritually guided to pivot my business and develop a mindfulness process that would help women step into their divine power and serve from the heart. I tapped into everything I've learned over the past twenty years as a successful multi-business owner and embraced a new direction. As a teacher of transformation, I now take women in business on a four-step journey to transform their energy from attracting lack to aligning with high-money vibrations that will see an abundance of cash and dream clients flow in with divine ease. My team and I uncover your authentic personality style and signature colours and then harmonize your online presence with your personal brand. We also help you identify and explore your ideal client, creating a rock-solid foundation for your divine business.

There are so many talented, gifted women who are ready

to serve with heart but find themselves paralyzed by all the steps necessary to set up and run a business. If you are nodding your head reading this, then we would love to support you. As Marie Forleo says, "The world needs that special gift that only you have."

Life will never be the same post-pandemic, and our ability to step into our feminine power will depend on whether we are choosing resistance or acceptance. Our willingness to shift our perspective and see the good available to us is what will allow us to dance with life and thrive.

www.BecomeaHighValueWoman.com
Email: Moira@BecomeaHighValueWoman.com
Facebook: Become a High Value Woman
Instagram: @becomeahighvaluewoman

About Moira Cohn

Moira Cohn is the founder and CEO of Become a High Value Woman and lead developer of Transformative Language of Connection™. Knowing first-hand the power of cultivating self-confidence, she is deeply passionate about performing high-value mindset work and makeovers for female entrepreneurs ready to become the best versions of themselves. She brings her experience as a successful multi-business owner and image consultant as well as her counselling skills to divinely guide women from overwhelm to launching their sacred business.

After coming across so many women striving to break out into new versions of themselves but unsure of where to begin, Moira created a brand-new, proprietary communication method known as The Transformative Language of Connection™. T.L.C.™ is a simple process that helps women shift from confusion to confidence, strengthening their emotional intelligence and allowing them to better communicate their thoughts, feelings, and desires.

When she is not running her business, Moira enjoys the silly side of life, finding joy and laughter in almost anything. You can often find her watching animated Disney movies with the new love of her life or starting exciting adventures with her friends.

10

Be Unstoppable

By Brenda Smith

*"You cannot change
the circumstances, the seasons, or the wind,
but you can change yourself.
That is something you have charge of."*

Jim Rohn

Be Unstoppable

By Brenda Smith

I didn't start my business with the thought that I would one day have to completely transform it. Instead, Club Cat started as a way of pursuing my dream of working with animals for a living. As someone who struggles with depression, I used to hop from job to job in an effort to stay busy. I have been a manager in a house cleaning business and at restaurants, a partner in one of the largest janitorial firms, and a consultant/ trainer for job development programs. Eventually, as I began working on recovering from my depression, I realized that the only thing that consistently held my interest was cats. I first built a cattery so that I could breed Siamese cats, and while it was a wonderful experience in many ways, it wasn't profitable. I knew I still wanted to work with animals, and eventually I came up with the idea of a cat boarding business.

Right from the beginning, I knew that I wanted this to be a place where people would feel like their cats were still in a homey setting. Other boarding businesses in the area used cages like you would find at a vet's office – this gets the job done, but it feels very sterile and cold. In my boarding house there would be no cages, but rather comfortable themed rooms that offered warmth and security. And thus Club Cat was born. I modelled the house after a Victorian-style home owned by my great-uncle, and I built much of it myself in order to save on costs. There were French doors, wood floors, and cozy beds. Each cat would have their own room, and each one was decorated in a different theme – right down to the curtains on the windows. There were also double rooms for cats from the same household.

One of the defining aspects of Club Cat is the satire and humour – the miniature items and plays on words are what keep people laughing and coming back. For example, the Jungle Suite has the head of a plastic mouse mounted on the wall as a trophy. The Honeymoon Suite has a miniature rotating disco ball and a heart-shaped waterbed. I really enjoy making people laugh and seeing their expressions when they see these things. Historically, this has been how I create a connection with my clients.

In early 2020, I was building a brand-new high-tech addition to my business: a dome-shaped building I'm calling the Oasis. In addition to spacious suites, miniature fireplaces, and recliners, it would be equipped with livestreaming cameras so that cat owners can watch their pets while they are away. There would also be automatic feeders and waterers that the owners can control through an app, allowing them to interact with their pet and be reassured that the cats are being well cared for. I had also hoped to release a book about cats when I did the grand opening in June, but 2020 had other plans.

The COVID-19 pandemic arrived and the world turn on its head. Once the initial panic settled down and we all realized that this virus would be around for quite some time, it became clear that life as we knew it was going to change in a significant way. As much as I hate the phrase "the new normal," I believe that there is some truth to it. The tourism industry has been decimated, and it appears that the market has possibly changed forever. In order to stay relevant in this new era, it is time to redefine my vision for the future. Running a business is all about handling change, and the best way to do it is becoming as agile as possible.

In order to determine my options for pivoting my business, I needed to understand the unique needs of the marketplace today – one where people are largely limited to their homes and neighbourhoods. I needed to find a way to serve that market. What are people doing now that they weren't doing before? What are they doing more of? What services could I offer to meet the demands of this new market, and which ones would be lucrative enough to keep my business running? After some thought, I came up with seven potential ideas that I could explore.

The first pivot is to update my website and social media. I started off by looking at my website and evaluating its effectiveness. About ten years ago I had animated characters on my website, and the average time that people would spend looking at these characters was seven minutes. There were two different characters: Simon Catwell, who gave sarcastic answers, and the Catcierge, who was the polite one. Together, they answered frequently asked questions and explained hotel policies. The service became less effective when smartphones became the norm as the animations did not work on them

– this technology has since been updated and improved upon, but I have not yet brought these animations back. This was one potential area to explore, but I knew there was more I could do.

To get some inspiration for ways I could improve my website, I researched how other industries were changing their approach. I have historically done showings by holding an open house every Sunday, but that was no longer possible. After seeing how the real estate industry adapted the way they show homes, I came up with the idea of adding virtual tours of Club Cat and then doing Facetime showings. Hotels for humans often have 3D tours of their suites, and this also seems to be a great way to showcase the finer points in the cat rooms. Also, adding a live chat that is available during specified hours would be a great way to create a bond with new clients and maintain my relationships with the current ones.

Another option is strengthening my social media presence. Up until now, this has not been a high priority for me – I had enough customers to keep me busy, and the majority of them were in an older demographic and were not often on social media. However, people now spend more time on these platforms than on searching websites. My website currently does not link to my Facebook, Instagram, Twitter, LinkedIn, and TikTok accounts – another thing to update.

Social media is one area where I have already started to make changes. I updated my business Facebook page and invited more of my contacts to join, whether they had a cat or not. I've also added a section for cats and kittens I have for adoption. On occasion, I receive cats who have lost their owners as well as orphan kittens or pregnant moms. In the past, I had enough foot traffic that I did not have any difficulty placing these cats in permanent homes. Now that I have less people coming into my business, I have created a link to a livestreaming camera showcasing the available cats so that people will hopefully fall in love with them and adopt them.

Outside of Facebook, though, I am not utilizing these platforms to their full extent. One platform I am looking to expand my presence on is Instagram. This is a great place to post and view pictures and videos of kittens and cats – there seems to be a nearly endless supply of them. The reason why cat videos are so popular is multifaceted. One theory by viral expert Matt Smith is that because cats are so acrobatic, they are very entertaining when they jump around. They also appear to be oblivious to the fact that they are being filmed, which means they act completely naturally. The great part about Instagram is that there are plenty of cat pictures and videos to share if one doesn't have anything current to add. By increasing my presence on Instagram, I can drive traffic to my website and to the live feed from the hotel.

One interesting social media platform that exploded at the beginning of the pandemic is TikTok. It is much more casual than the other sites and seems to be mainly filled with people poking fun at themselves. Kids, parents, and grandparents all make videos based on challenges, which include songs and dances. And of course, there are animals too. I got hooked on an account that simply showed a man talking to his dog and then using another voice to have the dog answer him. As the year progressed, he added in two other dogs as well. It reminded me of the comic strips and various cartoons I had seen, including my own animated characters from the past.

These videos gave me an idea for my next pivot: getting creative and using what I have. TikTok provided the perfect opportunity to revive this part of my business and play right into the satire and humour that has always been at the core of Club Cat. I am now trying to turn my cats into a "staff" for the hotel. There is Simon Catwell the butler, Mz. Blanca White the executive mousekeeper, Tuffie the entertainment director, and Marley the groundskeeper/gardener. There is also Mr. Wong, senior lawyer at the White and Wong law firm, as well as his paralegal Susume. I see these characters as being my best ambassadors for all the social media platforms. I can put them up on one of the livestreaming cameras or use their avatars to answer FAQs or handle the live chat – after all, avatars are quite a bit easier to control than the actual cat! And once the boarding business increases again, I can have the characters interact with the guests for their owners' entertainment.

In a perfect world, I hope to have enough followers that I can get paid to showcase wares for pet-related businesses. Simon Catwell really wants to be an influencer while Marley wants to be a catnip tester.

On top of improving my online presence, another idea I came up with was to change the perceptions around who would use my business and why. Pets have generally benefited from the COVID-19 crisis. Many animals that were up for adoption have found homes as people look for comfort, and people have been spending more time with their pets – although whether all cats appreciate the increased attention is up for debate! With less people travelling, I tried convincing some clients that just because they can't go on vacation doesn't mean their cats shouldn't. Unsurprisingly, no one bought into this idea.

The final option I came up with was to diversify. I have attended many pet expos, cat shows, and trade shows selling cat items and promoting Club Cat, but I had shied away from doing an online store because of the expense. The technology needed to add this to the site wasn't as available back then as it is now. I have also thought about making an app that would allow clients to make changes and update their cats' medical and feeding regimes.

Once I identified my pivots, it was time to look at the feasibility of implementing these ideas. I could immediately discard the epic fail of cat staycations. Truth be told, I wasn't actually serious about that one!

The financial resources required to implement the website updates and the virtual tours are not insurmountable, but the skills and time are scarcer. I have decided to pursue this, and for now I have hired a skilled person to take on these tasks. This is not sustainable forever; I will need to become more proficient at managing my own social media. I realize that it is time to become a student again and start learning about creating social media content; fortunately, there are so many how-to videos and sites available. My best teachers are my grand-nieces and nephews, ages ten, twelve, and thirteen. They don't complicate things and are really enthusiastic. And as I am learning, I am creating a plan for how I will move forward. I know that I can prepare Facebook posts ahead of time and schedule them, as well as for Instagram and TikTok posts. Knowing how busy I can get, I plan to be ahead of schedule by thirty posts at all times.

Adding an e-commerce store to my website is not feasible at this time due to the expense of setting it up. Instead, I decided to start the Curiosity Shop on Amazon, eBay, and Shopify and promote the items on Instagram and Facebook. This allows me to test this market with minimal risk and time commitment, especially as I already have a reasonable amount of inventory in stock.

The Club Cat staff is what I feel will be the most beneficial to my business, and so this is going to be my main focus and will receive about one third of my time as it is something only I can do. I will use Oddcast or a similar service to create and share the animated characters until I finish my trial for this. If it goes how I intend, I will then set up my own animation and voice overs.

Even with all of these changes on the horizon, I am not compromising my original vision for Club Cat. The Oasis is still in the works – the grand opening is now scheduled for June 1, 2021, with the book being released shortly after. Satire and humour still stay at the centre of what I do, and I will now use these to attract customers through a variety of formats. The hotel will continue to offer comfort, warmth, and security to all its residents. Who we are at our core is not changing; we are simply growing and evolving with the times.

Any significant change comes with a lot of uncertainty. Will I be able to get enough followers on social media to turn potential clients to cash? Will Simon Catwell make it as an influencer? Will Marley receive unlimited catnip? What I have realized is that even though I have gotten very comfortable in my business over the last twenty-four years, I cannot just stay where I am. The world is always changing, and I have often told others that if your business is not growing, it is dying. Staying the same is putting yourself on the fast track to becoming a dinosaur. It's time for Club Cat 2.0.

If you find yourself in the same situation – facing an enormous shift in the way your business must operate – then don't get stuck wallowing in self-pity. Instead, take a step back and really look at what you have to offer. You don't have to start from scratch! Go over each piece of your business and see what you can do to adapt it for your new reality. Research what other people in similar industries are doing and use that as inspiration. And once you know how you want to move forward, don't be afraid to reach out to those around who are knowledgeable on the subject – or alternatively, hire someone who specializes in that area. The world will always change, and it is only by embracing this change that we can become unstoppable.

About Brenda Smith

Brenda has been a lifelong cat lover. As a child, she regularly collected cats from the neighbourhood and brought them home, only for her mother to put them back outside at night so they could return to their owners.

Brenda has had many careers over the years, but the only thing that ever held her attention was cats. After years of trying to escape her depression by changing jobs and locations, she decided to stop running and really listen to what she wanted to do. She started a cattery at the farm she was living on in 1996 followed by Club Cat Hotel in 1997, guided by the facility rating programs from the Cat Fanciers Association and the International Cat Association.

Club Cat has been a true lifesaver for Brenda and has brought many new friends into her life. It was featured twice on a program called *Pet Friends*, on the news with Dave Gerry of City TV, and in the book *Cats I Have Known and Loved* by renowned Canadian author Pierre Berton. It is partnered with her Diplocat service, through which cats can be transferred to and from the boarding facility in a limousine.

www.clubcat.ca
Facebook: Club Cat Hotel Corp
Instagram: @Clubcat9 • **LinkedIn:** Brenda Smith
TikTok: Club Cat Hotel Corp

11

Evolution through Empowerment

By Heather Dodd

*"I wish that more women realized that helping
another woman win, cheering her on,
praying for her, or sharing a resource with her does
not take away from the blessings coming to them.
In fact, the more you give, the more you receive.
Empowering women doesn't come from selfishness,
but rather from selflessness."*

Selene Kinder

Evolution through Empowerment

By Heather Dodd

Success was never something that came easily for me. I grew up in a family that had very little money and was a victim of sexual abuse and childhood bullying due to obesity. I was constantly judged by my appearance. I became gifted in making deep connections with women, probably because I knew trauma and could connect with others over their own experiences. It was these connections that brought me to the start of Refresh Evolution, and to empowering women to own their own businesses.

In January of 2014, my marriage came to an end. I was devastated, and I quickly realized my situation was going to be as easy to crawl away from as one of those sticky glue traps that mice get caught in. I had sold my licensed daycare and decided to put the money into improving my home – but it wasn't actually my home. It was my soon-to-be-ex-husband's mother's home; I wasn't even on title. All I had was a Hyundai Santa Fe that I owed more money on than it was worth and four beautiful children (ages fifteen, twelve, seven, and four) to whom I owed a life.

By the spring of 2014 I was living on child tax benefits, child support, and Kraft Dinner. It wasn't pretty. I had secured a four-bedroom townhouse rental and was trying to find work, but it was difficult. My work experience wasn't a limiting factor – I'd already owned several businesses by this point – it was my lack of education. Every employer was looking for a four-year degree because it showed commitment, and all I had was an eighteen-month degree in pharmacy technology that had more dust on it than an Egyptian tomb.

The other challenge I faced as a woefully un-showered single mother of four was childcare. It was very difficult to find a job that would allow me to only work during school hours, and thirteen dollars an hour wasn't even enough to pay for a sitter and a gourmet meal of chicken nuggets.

I'll never forget the moment I was introduced to the idea that I could potentially buy my own laser hair removal machine. Eyelash extensions had recently arrived in the beauty industry, and on occasion I'd get them done. One day, I arrived at the salon and saw this crazy R2D2-looking thing in the hallway. I asked the owner, Shannon, what it was, and she told me they had started to offer laser hair removal. Immediately, I started asking her questions about licensing and training. Shannon gave me every single piece of advice and knowledge she had, and when she finished, she wrote down the name and phone number of the laser rep. That information sent me on a trajectory of empowerment that would impact my life, and my children's lives, forever.

Sometimes women won't share their knowledge for fear of competition. It's been ingrained in us that there are very few spots at the top for women, like there is some imaginary ceiling that lowers every single time we have a baby. I think this is because up until recently, there have been very few female mentors who have taken equal positions and earnings in the corporate world. I've always thought that if we just opened our arms up and collaborated like men do – like Shannon did for me – we'd be unstoppable! I am so humbled and grateful for that day in the salon when another woman was able to give me a gift that changed my life, and I've made it my mission to share, mentor, and help other women in any way I can.

After talking with Shannon, I was excited. I had the million-dollar idea: I was going to buy a laser and become a laser technician. But hold on, I'm the million-dollar idea girl who's as broke as a tooth fairy in a house full of meth heads. How the hell was I going to get my hands on that laser? I needed information. I picked up the phone, dialled the number, and talked my way to a potential leasing agent who would be able to give me all my financial options – as if I had any besides winning the lottery.

I learned that I would need $28,000 or at least some credit; I had neither. But the amazing thing about financing medical equipment is that if you can afford your current situation – leasing a building or renting a room or whatever it may be – leasing agents will take your return on investment (ROI) into consideration. This means you can build a business case around how much you will make and essentially use what you think your profits will be to finance the equipment. What they won't let you finance is the down payment, which is typically one fifth of the total amount. In my case, I had to come up with $6,000.

While I was building my business plan in order to acquire the loan, it occurred to me that I was missing one key component. Where would I put the laser? Leasing a space would require several thousand dollars per month, and my expenses were already just about maxing out my budget. So, I started to look at my current living situation. The townhouse I rented had a bedroom in the basement that was right beside the front door, which was currently the living quarters of my now sixteen-year-old son, Greyson. I started to visualize a laser room in the basement of my home. There was a bathroom, a bedroom, and street access. It was perfect! But where would I move my son to? And then, like the Grinch, an idea came to me and I started to smile. This house had a garage that was way too small to park a car in; I would make it into a makeshift bedroom. It would be awesome, like his own miniature condo. Heck, it even had a fridge!

The next morning, after Greyson went off to school, I started dismantling his bed and dragging all his belongings into the garage. When he returned home, he wasn't overly thrilled with his forced move – that is, until he realized that he and his friends now had unlimited access to the outside world. No alarm would sound when he opened the door, so he could come and go as he pleased without anyone even knowing he was away.

Great news! My financing was approved with my current business model – contingent on the down payment, of course, which was another roadblock. How the hell would I find six thousand dollars? I was still completely broke and didn't have anyone I could borrow money from. So, I started selling things – clothes that the kids had grown out of, old jewellery, things that we didn't need any more (or at least, that I told myself we didn't). I also had a friend who had just bought a strip club, and he let me work in his business a few nights a week serving drinks and bartending from 7:00 p.m. until 2:00 a.m. He didn't pay me an hourly wage, just allowed me to keep all my tips, and I hustled to make as much money as I could. It took me forty-five days to come up with the down payment, and during that time I had my sixteen-year-old son and my twelve-year-old daughter to babysit the other two boys, who were five and eight at the time – unpaid, of course. The job mostly fell on my daughter, Hope. She would bathe her brothers, feed them, and put them to bed, and she never complained. Today, she is nineteen years old, lives on her own, and works for me in one of my clinics. She's determined, kind, and has an amazing work ethic. She's probably one of the most responsible nineteen-year-olds I have ever met, and I'm so very proud of her.

I'll never forget the day the laser was delivered – I have a picture of me hugging my very own R2D2. I had posted it to Facebook in the hopes that my friends would see I had a laser and come to me for treatments, but now it serves as a humbling reminder about how and where I started. My past has not defined me, destroyed me, or defeated me; it has only strengthened me.

That first month, my friends supported me. They sent their friends to see me, and I started to build my business. I needed to make $700 to pay for the lease on my laser, and I made close to $1,000. This was the first time I'd taken a deep breath in close to a year. My plan was working.

Of course, there were a few kinks to work out, including the awkwardness of doing full-body laser hair removal in my home with my kids around. I remember talking to one of my best friends, Ashley, about what kind of treats it was going to take to keep my kids from fighting upstairs while I removed pubic hair in the basement. It turned out Ashley had just visited a cool little place in Pitt Meadows called Sour Apple Salon for a pedicure. She said they offered so many personal services but she didn't think laser was one of them, and she encouraged me to call them up and see if I could do laser out of one of their rooms. That conversation was pivotal for me; without Ashley's recommendation, I wouldn't be where I am today. This rings true for almost every relationship I have with my female friends. They have all supported me and propelled me to be better or do better, and I am eternally grateful for them.

Of course, I took my best friend's advice and called Sour Apple. I then met with Diana and Rachel, two amazing women who took a chance on me. This is really where Refresh Evolution was born. At first I gave these women a percentage of my sales in exchange for rent and reception services, but by my third month in business I was handing over more than $3,000 per month. I renegotiated my terms with them and settled on a $1,000-per-month room rental. Diana didn't have to do that for me – I was contractually bound to a percentage share contract – but she was fair, and she understood how hard I was working to support my kids. I always tell anyone who asks that Sour Apple Salon is where I got my start. Without them, without the time and space they gifted me, my business would never have flourished like it did.

After being at Sour Apple for about eight months, I realized that many of my customers were coming to the end of their laser hair removal sessions. In order to keep them coming back, I needed to offer another service. I researched many, many machines and settled on Venus Freeze skin tightening. I leased the machine and scheduled an event where I sold discounted packages and sessions to my current clients. My customers were the absolute best. They believed in me and trusted my opinion, and that in turn gave me such a sense of belonging and security. Making them feel good about themselves and helping them to feel beautiful was what I lived for.

I'll never forget that event. I made $25,000 – the most money I had seen at once in my entire life. I was so excited and so grateful. I used part of this money to book my mom a trip to Vegas for her sixtieth birthday. My mom is the hardest working woman I've ever known, and I have so much respect for her. She basically raised four kids on her own, often working two jobs to make ends meet, and gave freely of everything she had. Without her love and support, without being witness to her hard work ethic, I wouldn't be where I am today.

I was well on my way to success when I met my current husband. I was working out of Sour Apple during the day and moving my skin tightening machine to Mission three evenings a week to give treatments to my friend's customers out of her salon. Remember the eyelash extensions? The technician, Stacy, ended up becoming a very good friend of mine, and she set me up with her customers and allowed me to use her space for a small commission. It was during this time that my boyfriend, now husband, gave me the best business advice that I have ever received. Kev watched me break my back day in and day out, working all day and then slinging Venus Freeze at night. Kev was already a very successful businessman, and he could see the mistake I was making. He said, "Heather, you're doing this all wrong. If you keep going the way you are, you will always be a slave to your business. The moment you will find true success is when you can build a business or a team that runs independently of you." That one piece of advice is what grew Refresh Evolution exponentially – well, that and Kevin's support. He was always there for me, he constantly built me up, and he even partnered with me on my second clinic. He believed in me like no one else ever had, except for maybe my mom.

After Kev's advice, I have to admit that for a while all I heard was "you're doing it wrong." I'm the type of person who would swallow my blood before swallowing my pride. However, I eventually came around to the idea that I needed staff, and so I set about finding them. One of my first hires was Patricia, a single mom who'd just moved her family back to Canada from South Africa. She is a go-getter, but in a much softer way than I am. We complimented each other perfectly, and she became my right-hand woman, so to speak. Trish started as a laser tech, then managed both of my clinics, and is now working in franchise integration and support. Without Trish, there would be no Refresh Evolution. I love her like a sister, and I am humbled by her devotion to me and to our business.

Shortly after I assembled a team of three more technicians, Sour Apple asked me to leave. To be fair, I had been there almost three years at that point, and I had far outgrown that room. I discovered there was a unit for lease one block down, so I called the number, negotiated the lease, and built my first stand-alone clinic over the next three months. With me opening just down the street, my customers didn't have to travel far and would continue to come to me.

The last year that I was at Sour Apple, Kevin and I partnered to open a second Refresh Evolution clinic. We secured a space in a hair salon in Port Moody called Angelos, and that business grew very quickly. In March of 2019, two years after opening, we moved the Port Moody location into its own stand-alone clinic, where it still is today.

Sometime during 2018, we decided to franchise the clinics. What a labour of love. To this day, it's the most difficult, expensive, time-consuming thing I have ever done, and also the most rewarding. It was two long, hard years before I sold my first franchise – a franchise is just a plan and a system until you actually have a franchisee. There were many failed attempts, financing that fell through, and hundreds of thousands of dollars spent in lead generation and franchise disclosure documents. It was the closest I have ever come to throwing in the towel and admitting defeat; even Kevin was starting to rethink the whole plan. Then I was given a gift, and her name was Kait.

Kait purchased the Pitt Meadows clinic and was set to take over on April 1, 2020. Then, Covid hit hard. By mid-March, a pandemic had been declared and all personal service businesses had been ordered to close. I could not lose this deal. It wasn't even about the money; I couldn't lose Kait. She was kind, driven and qualified. There was no better person to own the first Refresh Evolution franchise. I offered to pay all the expenses and rent for the business until she could open up again, and she trusted that we'd get through this together. That was a lot of trust.

I've never been one to just sit by and let things happen to me. I had to figure out how to pay the bills and keep both businesses afloat, so about five days into the closure I started to sell our in-store skin care products over Facebook and Instagram. I literally went from CEO/founder to delivery driver – probably the biggest demotion of my life – but it opened the door to a massive pivot for our businesses. Selling and delivering these skincare products was so successful that we created a customer-facing website for online purchasing, which became a brand-new revenue stream. This pivot didn't just help us survive, it helped us succeed!

When I think back to the evolution of my businesses, there is one quote by Robert H. Schuller that rings true: "Tough times never last, but tough people do." Tough times will come, and they will make you reinvent, recreate, shift and change. The secret to change is to focus all your energy not on fighting the old, but on building the new. And when we come together and lift each other up, we create a ripple of empowerment that will last for generations to come.

About Heather Dodd

Heather Dodd has successfully built, managed, and sold many businesses over the past twenty-five years and is considered an expert in the field of start-ups, business consulting, and sales. Her motivation to create Refresh Evolution came from her passion to empower women who are looking to become financially independent and to make positive visual changes on a very personal level. Since 2014, Refresh Evolution has grown into a full-service medical aesthetic clinic offering injectables, laser hair removal, and skin rejuvenation. They currently have two clinical locations, one in Pitt Meadows and one in Port Moody, and will be expanding with a third clinic in the fall.

Franchising Refresh Evolution was the ultimate goal for Heather as it offered a way to expand her work by managing growth and sales through a franchise model. She also believes that "a rising tide lifts all boats" and saw this as another opportunity to encourage and facilitate success among women in business. Refresh Evolution Franchise Corporation, whose head office is located in Maple Ridge, offers a unique franchise opportunity in the rapidly growing medical aesthetics industry. For those who want to know more, please visit the franchise website below.

www.refreshevolution.com
www.refreshevolutionfranchise.com

12

The Lessons Found in Topes

By Anita Voth

*"It's a dangerous business, Frodo,
going out your door. You step onto the road,
and if you don't keep your feet, there's no knowing
where you may be swept off to."*
J.R.R. Tolkien, The Lord of the Rings

The Lessons Found in Topes

By Anita Voth

Twenty-two years ago, I sold my adventure travel company, GAP Adventures (now known as G Adventures), put all my belongings in storage, packed up the kids and my husband into our Westfalia camper van, and headed south to Mexico from Toronto, Canada. It had long been a dream of ours to spend an extended time in Latin America, and now this dream was finally coming true. It was the best of times, it was the worst of times. We spent six months in Mexico, and it took a while to get used to the new rhythm of life. We moved fairly quicky as we made our way there but slowed down once we arrived, often spending anywhere from a few days to several weeks in one part of the country or another. The kids were one and three years old, and between nursing, playing, and finding things to keep them busy, we explored all that Mexico had to offer

– unless the van was broken down, in which case we would spend weeks on end in a campground waiting for parts or for a local mechanic to fix it.

One of my most vivid memories from this trip were the topes. These oversized speedbumps could be found anywhere, anytime, and could be either raised or indented. Sometimes, if we were paying attention, we would see them coming well in advance. Sometimes, we saw them last minute – one of us would yell "TOPE" at the top of our voice and my husband would slam on the brakes to avoid bottoming out. Sometimes we would hit it hard, which might be one of the reasons we were waiting for parts so often.

Since then, I have come to see these topes as a metaphor for my life. Over the last fifty-four years, there have been times I have seen topes coming and have been able to plan and change course. There have also been times when I saw the tope coming at the last minute and had to pivot quickly and adjust my course in a less comfortable way. And then there are those times when life seems good, I am feeling all on track, and then the tope appears seemingly out of nowhere. I have taken many personal development courses in the last fifteen years and learned so much about how to purposefully make changes and plan my life, but nothing can prepare you for those sudden curveballs that are completely out of your control. The only thing to rely on in those times is your inner strength and your ability to accept the situation as it is.

Fast forward twenty-two years and I once again found myself in Mexico. This time, I was alone – the kids were grown up and I was divorced. The topes, however, were the same. Some things never change.

I was in Mexico for what was supposed to be two months to take some time away, reflect on life, enjoy the sun and sea, and wind down. It had been a crazy eighteen months. I had moved in with my fiancé and his two teenage boys – need I say more? In addition, my fiancé and I were both working from home because of COVID-19 and the boys were around 24/7. I'd had my first taste of being an empty nester the year prior after my children had both begun living on their own, so this felt a bit like going backwards – not to mention losing one of my biggest clients and most of my income because of the pandemic. Navigating this took all my energy, especially as I had no control over much of it. I needed a break! So, off to Mexico I went.

The first week I was there felt great. I was staying at a beautiful condo with ocean views, a pool, and very safe health regulations in place. I discovered little shops to buy my food and cooked simple, healthy, delicious meals. I was still working from home, but I was able to set my own pace.

During the second week I relaxed into my new routine, knowing I had five more weeks to go. I then started a 10-week program using a book called The Presence Process and quickly began to experience breakthroughs. This book details a step-by-step process for creating wholeness and wellness in our lives by taking responsibility for our perceptions. I had done this program several times before, and it was great to see that some of the old things I had worked through previously were no longer coming up for me. However, there's always new layers to heal! Also, this was the first time doing this process after taking my neuro-linguistic programming (NLP) courses – more on that later – and I had new tools to work with. For example, by using a technique called "Timeline" in conjunction with the book exercises, I was able to heal negative emotions in a matter of minutes.

This trip was the perfect place for healing; sometimes, I

had to pinch myself to believe I was actually there, enjoying the ocean view, the sounds of waves easing me into sleep each night. I was able to practice the breathing techniques from the program while sitting on my balcony and watching whales swim by, which was so cathartic and relaxing. One day I went kayaking, and I saw a whale giving birth in the water as I was paddling by. I felt so honoured and blessed to be part of nature in this way.

There has always been something inside me that feels at home in Latin America. The smells, the sounds, the language, and the culture all felt so familiar even before I had ever been there. This was where I belonged – at least for the next two months.

Of course, I had once again noticed the topes upon arrival. Julie, my employer, had picked me up at the airport, and we came across many of them as we drove to my condo. Some of them seemed to appear out of nowhere as we were chatting and catching up, and she would have to slam on the brakes. In those moments, I was right back where I had been twenty-two years ago. I had driven these same streets before and had even taken pictures of the same statues on the Malecon in Puerto Vallarta.

Part of why I chose to come to this part of Mexico was to have in-person meetings with Julie, but as we all know, things do not always go according to plan. Within a few days of my arrival, she discovered that she had to immediately return to Canada for two weeks. Okay, that's not too bad; we would still have three weeks together when she returned. Little did I know that a few days after her departure, Prime Minister Justin Trudeau would announce that all flights in and out of Mexico were to be cancelled until May (with less than 48 hours' notice), and that soon all international travellers would need to quarantine in a hotel upon arriving in Canada until the results of their Covid test came in. This would cost approximately $2,000.

Once again, I was brought back in time to my previous trip to Mexico. My family and I were in Oaxaca and had to decide whether to continue to Guatemala, which involved travelling over a mountain range, or turn around and head back to Canada. Our six-month visa was going to expire in ten days, so we had to leave Mexico at least for a day to renew our visa before we could continue our travels – and soon. Our original plan had been to get to Guatemala, but with all the breakdowns and delays, getting there had taken longer than we had expected. We discussed and meditated and decided what the hell, let's go for it. But after about thirty minutes on the road, the van started smoking and sputtering. We knew it would never make it over the mountain range, so we turned around and headed back. My consolation prize was buying lots of Mexican pottery and bringing it home to decorate my house.

And now, here I was again. I had just gone to my favourite pottery store to buy a few things I could bring home, and I had a decision to make: stay two months longer than planned, or go home without achieving my plan – with the consolation prize of more pottery!

This time I was older and wiser, and I had definitely learned a few things over the past two decades. One of those lessons was staring me right in the face: things don't keep happening to you without there being something you need to learn from it. And so, my process began. I cried, felt disappointed, felt ripped off, felt angry, and questioned my decision-making abilities. Why had I decided to come here in the middle of a pandemic? Was it the wrong decision in the first place? And then it hit me. That is just life! I knew who I was, and that is someone who is not afraid to take risks (or at least won't let fear stop me) and who knew what I needed for my own health and wellbeing. I needed to go to Mexico, and I did; what happened after that was out of my control. I had taken a risk by going, and I know many people judged me for that choice. But I had been here before, and I would not live my life regretting the things I did not do.

Would I change who I am or deny what I knew to be right for me? No. Not this time. As a wife and mother, I had made so many compromises, and I would make many of them again. But now, at this time in my life, it was time to put myself first. Accepting myself and acknowledging that I had done the right thing for me gave me so much comfort in that moment.

As I shared in a recent podcast interview, I have learned to hold my hands out, palms up, and hold my plans and desires loosely. I am confident that I will manifest the things I need in my life at the right time. Forcing them is not always the right way for me; I just allow them to happen when the timing is right and in the way that life brings them to me. Even though I may not understand the timing or the reasons in the moment – even though I can't always see the good in it until much later – I have learned to trust that it will come.

I found out about the cancelled flights and new regulations on a Friday, and by Wednesday I'd bought a new ticket home to the tune of $1,100 and accepted the fact that there would be no meetings with Julie or time to myself or any of the things I was needing and enjoying. I could have chosen to stay in Mexico, but that would have cost me a lot more with no guarantee that the hotel quarantine would not still be in effect at the end of it. This hurt. I was frustrated and angry, but mostly I was sad. I had hoped to be writing this chapter from my Mexican condo, sitting on the balcony overlooking the ocean with the sound of waves as my music. Instead, I am sitting in a chair in Pitt Meadows hoping for a break in the clouds so that I can see the sun, with mountains as my backdrop instead of the warm sea. This too is part of life. Yes, this tope did a bit of damage, but I am healing and finding other ways to have quiet alone time.

Despite not getting to do everything I had planned, my trip was not in vain. The short time I was there gave me a bit of the break I needed, and it also gave me ideas for the future, though I don't know how they will all play out yet. I have also learned patience and acceptance. My hands are held open, and my dreams will not be reduced to the size of where life is at now.

This is not the first time I received the lesson that life does not always go as planned. In 2004, I received a call from my parents early one morning saying that my thirty-six-year-old sister, a mother of three young kids, had gone for a walk late the night before and never returned. She lived on a 100-acre farm in Ontario which bordered forestry land, so that is where the search started. One month later, her body was found in a pond on a golf course which also bordered their property. Nothing could have prepared me for this situation. My life became suddenly different; if that could happen, then anything could.

While this changed my life forever, it also laid the preparation for the idea that as much as we feel that we control our lives, we don't. Accepting that as fact immediately eliminates half of the battle. Instead of looking for ways that things could have been done differently, which means living in the past, I have found ways of looking at my life as it is right now and making decisions that can create peace and acceptance. Studying NLP has been a huge part of my growth and has helped me learn to live in the present and accept things without judgment. It has led me to be curious about people and about the situations I come across instead of immediately turning to attack, pain, and judgment. I am still learning these skills and sometimes need to be reminded of them, but I can already see so much change in my mindset and belief systems.

My fiancé and I took the first level of the course together, and then I continued on to get my Master Practitioner level. This has given us so many tools to build a solid foundation in our relationship, and it has helped me in my career as well as in all my family relationships. Most of all, it has helped me live a more peaceful life and allowed me to make decisions I know to be right for me without putting that on anyone else.

It has also led me to share this knowledge with others in the form of a course called Identity By Design, created by Emma McNally and Lynn Robinson. No matter what point in life you are at or what changes come your way – such as divorce, retirement, career change, pandemic, marriage, and more – the concepts you learn in this course will help you to navigate change in a way that keeps you at the core, like a deeply-rooted tree that can withstand being blown in the wind. Its concepts are so foundational that anyone at any stage of life can benefit from them; I personally used concepts from this course to help me work through having to suddenly cut my trip short and not receiving what I had planned. I teach this one-day workshop in a group setting so that people can pair off or work in small groups in order to share some of their learnings and stories for everyone to grow from. It is available online in small Zoom groups or in-person with groups of four to fifteen people. I am also hoping to include it in an upcoming retreat, so stay tuned!

Topes will always be present in our lives, and we won't always see them coming. However, we can take steps to put ourselves in the best mindset possible and give ourselves tools to navigate these unexpected changes. So, I'd like to finish off by sharing a few points you can use to help shift your focus to build a more positive and peaceful life.

1. Awareness: You have to be aware of your emotions – of how you feel about your situation. This is only the first step, though! We have to be careful we don't stop at awareness. Some people get stuck in this stage and never move forward.

2. Identity: Most people identify with the roles they play or the titles they hold. You are more than the roles you play. Understand that your role is not your true identity.

3. Beliefs: Look at what might be holding you back from living life to the fullest. There may be negative emotions or limiting beliefs you hold that you're not even aware of. To move forward, you have to let go of the past.

4. Experiences: This is about looking at the experiences you want to have in your future versus only focusing on goals you want to achieve. When you focus only on your goals, you become so caught up in reaching one target and then the next that you miss the moment-by-moment experiences – you miss your life. You forget about celebrating the successes and, more importantly, living in the present, in the now. Focus on enjoying the journey.

Sometimes, even small changes in our thinking can create big results in our life. The world needs more positive thinking, and my belief is that by being the best person I can be, the energy from this will resound to influence those around me in a positive way. And when those topes come my way, I'll be ready to overcome them.

About Anita Voth

Anita is the mother of three wonderful young adult children and has been a business owner for over thirty years. From starting a business in adventure travel in Toronto, Ontario to currently owning her own business as a financial advisor and small business administrator in Vancouver, BC, she would sum herself up as a "humanitarian with a sense of adventure."

Over the past thirteen years, Anita has had the privilege of teaching; co-hosting a radio series on family and finance; being the annual financial "expert" for the Total Makeover Challenge; and teaching personal development seminars. In the last decade, she has sat on several non-profit boards including Shape Your World Society (SYWS) and has volunteered with SYWS for the past eight years. Anita is a certified NLP Master Practitioner and has spent the last fifteen years focusing on her own personal development through a variety of courses and programs.

With a clear but simple mission of helping and inspiring others, Anita is a proud personal development speaker that is known for making a memorable impact, and by providing the right tools and knowledge, she helps people unleash their potential.

www.anitavoth.com
Facebook: Anita Voth • **Instagram:** @anitakvoth

13

Relentless Resilience

By Denise Mai

*"Your present circumstances don't
determine where you can go,
they merely determine where you start."*

Nido Qubein

Relentless Resilience

By Denise Mai

What does it mean to be resilient? To overcome our challenges rather than letting our failures derail our dreams? What could we accomplish if we had the strength to persevere? We don't get to choose the cards we are dealt in life, but we CAN choose how we play our hand. By sharing my story, I hope to help you discover how resilience can build your confidence and ultimately change the course of your life for the better.

We all experience adversity in one way or another – life threatening illness, the loss of a loved one, physical abuse, bullying, bankruptcy, the list goes on. The question is, how do you choose to face these challenges? Are you a victim of your circumstances, or do you utilize them to fuel your way to success?

My story of resilience begins with my mom. She was born in Vietnam and fled her home country with her younger sister during the Vietnam War. She risked her life to escape, hoping for a brighter future. She paid four gold bars for passage on a boat; unfortunately, their boat broke down. My mom and her sister, along with 650 other refugees, were stranded in international waters for four days with barely any water, food, or resources. During this time, they were attacked and robbed by pirates, who came on board and stole any jewelry, gold, or valuables they could find. My mom had her watch stolen from her wrist, but she had wisely sewn her jewelry to the inside of her underwear so she was able to keep it concealed. The pirates even came back the next day for a second round. My mom lost some of her jewelry, but more devastating was losing her sister on the boat due to the harsh and treacherous conditions.

My mom has truly shown me what resilience means. She had me at the age of forty and became a single mom on welfare. I grew up in Chinatown, and I remember lining up for food at the food bank, having Christmas dinner at the Union Gospel Mission, and getting used clothing and toys from the Salvation Army. Looking back, though, I can see that my mother did the best she could with what she had. I knew we were poor, and that we didn't have much, but I still have many happy, loving memories with my mom.

When I was eight, I came home from school one day and saw a man sitting in the kitchen. My mom introduced him as my father – this was the day my stepfather came into my life. My dad took my mom and I in and treated me as his own daughter. He showed us unconditional love and relentless resilience, working at a restaurant twelve hours a day, six days a week to provide for us. Seeing my dad work so hard created a deep-rooted sense of resilience within me as well as a hard work ethic.

I got my first job at the tender age of ten, working once a week making sandwiches on a conveyor belt with my mom. We would wake up at 5:00 a.m. every Saturday, when it was pitch black outside, to take the bus to the sandwich factory two hours away. I missed out on many childhood activities, but this increased my independence and resilience. From that day on, I vowed to make my own money and become successful so that I would one day be able to provide for and give back to my parents.

The discipline and hard work ethic I built throughout my early years have played a vital role in my achievements throughout my life. They created a deep-rooted yearning for success that has driven me to get the most out of life.

When I turned eighteen, my father sold our home for $300,000. It was the worst timing – a year later, the housing market in Vancouver took off. We could've sold at double the value if he had only waited a few more years; this was the story of my dad's life. We moved into a tiny two-bedroom basement rental suite, only 550 square feet, and lived there for the next ten years. This was a pivotal decade for me. It was a dark and depressing time, and as a teenager, I was still finding myself. One day, I was comparing my life to others, especially to other women whom I strived to be – beautiful, smart, successful, and wealthy – and something snapped inside me. In that moment, I had a realization that would change the trajectory of my entire life. I realized that I would not let my present circumstances keep me from wanting more out of life. Instead, I would use this feeling of worthlessness as my fuel, pushing me to prove to the world that I can and will make something of myself.

I decided that the way I was going to achieve my goal was to get a corporate job and work on climbing the ladder. So, I pursued a university degree and worked retail jobs to cover my tuition. I never thought of myself as one of the smart ones – I was always an average student in my mind, getting an occasional A but mostly B's and C's. But despite my average grades, I was blessed with the opportunity to work for two Fortune 500 companies. However, after spending a few years in the corporate world, I realized that it wasn't for me. I didn't want to work 9-5 for the rest of my life, and most importantly, I did not want to have someone else dictating how much money I would earn each year. I wanted a job where the harder I worked, the more I would make – I was an entrepreneur at heart.

One day, I had lunch with the CEO of the Fortune 500 company I was working for at the time, and he suggested I get into real estate. I was intrigued by the suggestion, but I thought to myself, *Who's going to trust a twenty-four-year-old with their million-dollar home?* I didn't have enough confidence in myself just yet.

Soon after, I received an opportunity to enter a contest to sell ad spaces in a coffee newsletter, with the grand prize being a trip anywhere in the world. I entered with one of my best friends, and we decided to target realtors. We booked four appointments for the next day, but then my friend called me at 3:00 a.m. and said she wouldn't be able to make it as she'd been arguing with her boyfriend all night. I called the owner of the newsletter to ask him what I should do, and he said, "Denise, I believe in you. You can do it." So, I ended up meeting the realtors by myself. Long story short, I ended up beating out twenty other teams and winning the contest on my own. This proved to me that I could sell, which meant I could succeed as a realtor.

I got my license in 2010, and today I've been ranked as a top 1% performing agent with over $350M in sales. I am the owner of ten properties, and I'm financially free. I tell you this not to impress you, but to impress upon you that this little girl from the rough side of Chinatown was able to achieve more than I ever could've imagined.

Of course, I didn't get to where I am today just by becoming a realtor – it took relentless hard work. I was hungry and passionate, which meant I worked tirelessly six to seven days a week, driving one to two hours out of the city to show clients properties, doing whatever it took to create the income I wanted and make something out of myself. I had an insatiable attitude for personal growth, and still do, which propelled me faster towards success. I had an open mind, was coachable, and learned to get my own ego and limiting beliefs out of the way. This wasn't easy to do, because it meant facing myself and taking responsibility for my own actions. Doing so much personal growth allowed me to unravel the layers that were holding me back from my potential and, most importantly, to heal the wounds from my childhood.

When I first got started in real estate, I joined a team so that I could receive support and gain experience quickly. I quickly got my feet wet and did everything in my power to close the leads sent to me by my team leader. I also sought out different mentors, guidance, and training so that I could improve my skills. I met with two real estate coaches who were not a good fit for me, but then I found my mentor, Mike Ferry. Through his coaching, I was able to propel myself forward in my career.

In my third year, I purchased my first property and moved my parents and I from our tiny rental into a two-bedroom apartment. This was a special time in my life as I was finally able to give back to my parents.

I broke off from the team in my fourth year, and this really tested me as an entrepreneur and business owner. I thought about getting a second job because I felt the pressure of my mortgage and bills, but luckily I didn't give up and continued pushing through. As a result, my fifth year in real estate saw me catapulting to the top 1% of realtors in Greater Vancouver, placing me 32 out of 14,000 agents. I attribute this success to many factors such as hiring a coach, surrounding myself with top producing agents by joining a mastermind, and always having a growth-oriented mindset. I bought my first investment property in 2014, and I intend to keep expanding my real estate portfolio. On the advice of my mentor, I have decided to buy one property a year for the next ten years, paying off the mortgages by renting the properties.

Sometimes, I look back and wish that I had become a realtor earlier on – perhaps then I would have been able to help my dad make a better decision. However, if I had not gone through a decade of living in that dark, depressing basement suite, I wouldn't have learned what it feels like to be at rock bottom both emotionally and physically. This experience gave me a powerful motivation to succeed so that I could give back to my parents and provide them with a happy retirement. I turned my struggles into my strength, and this mindset helped carry me towards my goals and dreams.

I could have easily been a victim of my circumstance, a victim to the cards I was dealt in life. But resilience is infectious, and I was fortunate enough to see this exemplified in my parents. Some may say the challenges they faced were harder and more difficult than others, but in my eyes, the adversity they went through and the perseverance I've seen in them has made me into who I am today. They truly showed me what relentless resilience is, and they are my role models for life.

However, I'm not saying that the only way to learn resilience is by witnessing it in others; it can be taught and strengthened with the right training and conditions, giving us better protection against hardship and a buffer in difficult times. Resilience is more than a skill, it's an adaptation. So, I want to leave you with four action items that will help build your resilience and confidence.

The first thing to do is change your perspective! As Dr. Wayne Dyer says in one of my favourite quotes, "When you change the way you look at things, the things you look at change." When you adjust your perspective, you can see opportunities instead of obstacles. This is a way to reframe the way you see the world around you. Personally, I choose to look at my life not through a victim perspective, but rather from the perspective of being faced with challenges I could overcome. When it came to breaking out of the lot I was born into, the odds were stacked against me – just sixteen percent of children who grow up in poverty manage to become economically successful adults. But through hard work and determination, I was able to overcome my obstacles and achieve my dreams.

The second step is choosing your response. Remember, we all experience bad days, and we all go through our share of crises. However, we have a choice in how we respond: we can panic and react negatively, or we can remain calm and find a solution. Your reaction is always up to you. When I was faced with the decision during that ad contest to either move forward with those meetings or give up, I decided to push through my fear (with a bit of motivation from my boss). This led me to a path of opportunity that eventually brought me to becoming a realtor. If I had panicked and dropped out of the contest, I wouldn't be where I am today.

It is also important to learn from your mistakes and failures. Every mistake has the power to teach you something important, so don't stop searching until you've found the lesson in every situation. Also, make sure that you understand the idea of "post-traumatic growth" – there can be real truth in the saying, "What doesn't kill you makes you stronger." Whenever I am faced with failure, I always ask myself, "What can I learn from this? What are my options?" These questions turn you away from the blame game and allow you to focus on the good that might come from the situation.

Finally, you need to find a sense of purpose. Growing up in poverty and seeing my parents go through so many hardships gave me my purpose: to achieve success so that I could give back to my parents, and so that I could provide my children with a better life. Having this sense of purpose is what drove me to overcome every obstacle and constantly strive to do better.

You cannot protect yourself from every hardship in life. What you *can* do is improve your capacity to endure the hardships, to recover more quickly, and most importantly, to KNOW and have confidence that it is always possible to overcome adversity. You are stronger than you know! By developing your resilience, you gain the power to overcome any obstacles in your way and live the life you've always imagined.

www.denisemai.com
Facebook: Denise Mai - Realtor
Twitter: @DeniseMaiRemax • **LinkedIn:** Denise Mai
Instagram: @denisemai_realestate

About Denise Mai

Denise Mai – a TEDx speaker, investor, and entrepreneur – is now on a mission to inspire others and leave a positive impact in their lives. From being raised in a poor immigrant family to self-made millionaire, she has turned her struggles into her greatest strengths. In her TEDx talk "How to build resilience as your superpower," she reveals that your circumstances do not dictate your future.

Denise holds a BBA in Communications from Simon Fraser University. She has worked with two Fortune 500 companies, Accenture and Johnson & Johnson, before becoming an award-winning top 1% realtor in Vancouver. She has been in real estate since 2010 and shares her knowledge with her clients to help them achieve their real estate goals and dreams. Today she owns multiple investment properties, and her passion for personal growth is leading her to create her own coaching company.

One of the values that Denise prides herself on is giving back to the community. One example of her community commitment is her participation in the Canadian Blood Services as a regular blood donor. In addition, Denise is the top donor to Children's Miracle Network in her office and has made significant donations to the Union Gospel Mission.

14

Finding My Way in a New Day

By Ruth Purves Smith

*"Love is what carries you, for it is always there,
even in the dark, or most in the dark,
but shining out at times like
gold stitches in a piece of embroidery."*
Wendell Berry

Finding My Way in a New Day

By Ruth Purves Smith

As winter came to a close, my road manager and I were gearing up for the beginning of the touring season. The Alberta tours with the Texan songwriters were booked. I had a month of medical acting work at the University of Calgary to gather some extra dough for fixing our transport. The Scottish publicist, an almost William Blake-like character known as Medicine Man, would be arriving at the end of May to start booking shows and mapping out the route for our Canada-wide tour. Once we were finished the shows in Alberta with the Texans, we would be travelling to Sydney, British Columbia, to begin the Auld Scotia to Nova Scotia *stravaig*.

These intrepid tours were all going to happen in an antique GMC motorhome called the Moose. This beloved vehicle had already traversed twenty-five American states, the Navajo

Nation, and much of Western Canada. It is a mobile radio/TV station, a home for wayward musicians, and a magic tour bus of musical adventure. It still has a carburetor. I like old things – a passion that began in my childhood.

A great deal of my upbringing was split between a circa-1800s woollen mill and the backwoods of the Canadian Rocky Mountains. In the 1970s, my father and step-mum had purchased the machinery from a couple of retired woollen mills that were being sold for scrap. The mill they crafted was, and still very much is, like a time warp into the days of the Industrial Revolution. The sights, sounds, and smells are the same as they were over 150 years ago, and this made for a labyrinth of wonder that filled my younger days.

While the woollen mill is situated in the rolling farmlands, my grandparents' ranch was in the Western foothills. I spent as much of my childhood there as I could. The horses, one of my greatest loves in life, were a magnet; my sister and I would often get in trouble for disappearing to the barns. Growing up at the ranch led to many years of working in the big horse outfits, where I would trail hundreds of miles on horseback as a cook and horse wrangler. The mechanical, physical, and tangible nature of this kind of life left me with little interest in things like computers. To this day, I have not played even one video game.

In addition to my passions for antiques and the outdoors, I also have a deep love of music. On and off for the past thirty-five years, I have led bands, presented innumerable live and recorded performances, and toured much of North America and the UK. I have independently released two critically acclaimed self-penned albums and am currently in the studio with a third. I have also worked for many years as an actor for the university and the legal society, portraying characters and scenarios to assist in testing, training, and education. All of this work has meant I was constantly on the road, in part because I live in a tiny hamlet on the vast Alberta prairie. The nearest amenity is twenty minutes away, and Calgary, the closest city, is about one and a half hours. There's not even a payphone here! Well, I guess there's actually no payphones anywhere anymore, but that shows you where my brain is at. I really have never had any aptitude for the internet, social media, or anything modern and technical. That was Medicine Man's domain. I played the songs, he broadcasted them.

So, back to the story. This was to be the biggest tour to date, and everything was really lining up. Oh, did I mention that it was the second week of March, 2020?

We all know what happened next. What started as a two-week shutdown soon turned to two months, which then turned to ... indefinitely? Live music was rapidly going by the boards. One by one, the dates for our shows were cancelled. All my work at the university was stopped, and every source of income I had disappeared. Nobody was coming from Texas, or Scotland, or even across the province. Now what?

Well, first I freaked out and grew six hundred tomato plants. Okay, it wasn't all tomato plants, but it was definitely panic planting! This is no small feat in Alberta. Plants take up a lot of space; require plenty of dirt, light, and water; and must be kept at a suitable temperature until spring fully arrives – usually about the end of May. There were grow lights to install, water troughs to assemble, and a greenhouse to be built. This was all keeping me very busy, but I still wanted to find a way to stay connected with my music and creative arts community.

Overseas, Medicine Man was doing his best to get performing artists to start livestreaming. Broadcasting in this way was a big part of what he did for us on the road. He eventually figured out how to set it up so an artist could stream from wherever they were to his Facebook page. It was a start. In the meantime, inspired by his efforts, I decided that I should read a little Edgar Allan Poe to the people one night. My theatrical side leans to the macabre, and a recitation of "The Cask of Amontillado" soon led to a daily livestream. At first I used a phone and a mirror, but before long I had two phones: one for a camera and one to see the video and comments. I was really streaming now! My tech savvy was surely coming along.

About a week into livestreaming, I agreed to start sharing my original music and the somewhat quirky show I was developing on Medicine Man's Facebook channel. In theory, this was a great idea. Because of the seven-hour time difference, I could do a livestream at 1:00 p.m. my time (8:00 p.m. for him) and it would not be too rushed for me to do my own broadcast later. However, the best laid plans sometimes go awry, and the challenges of livestreaming with a smartphone were rapidly revealing themselves. My stream was right at the kiddies' bedtime, and everyone was tuned in, anticipating a chapter of *Alice in Wonderland*. At a certain point, after a great deal of interweb kerfuffle, I became increasingly frustrated with Medicine Man, the phone, and the whole process. I hit the "finish livestream" button and proceeded to curse an epic blue streak – but as it turned out, I had NOT hit the "finish livestream" button. Instead, I had reversed the camera, and everyone was now seeing the dirty litter box as I streamed an episode that would make a pirate pale. This was the first and only show I did for my UK audience.

In spite of this setback, I continued on with my livestream, now dubbed "I Love Ruthie" by a close friend. I began to find more effective ways to manage my simple setup, and I was able to be relatively effective with my still very grassroots production qualities. I started to garner a small yet consistent online following and tips began trickling in.

Because of this virtual connection, I booked a few outdoor shows when the days turned into summer. People were craving live music, and so they braved all manner of weather to catch my limited live performances. Quite quickly, my tip jar began to fill with funds to start recording a new album. All this was happening during the pandemic, without me going more than an hour down the road. We independent musicians are well known for spending thousands of hours and dollars so we can drive one hundred miles and be paid fifty dollars to perform for three people, but it's not all glamour. This Internet thing was really looking not so bad after all – maybe the learning curve was worth it.

Not only was "I Love Ruthie" beginning to create a revenue stream, but, equally as important, it was also sustaining and building a community. This was a new virtual meeting place for me and my followers, and any likeminded person who came across us could join in as well. People who had never been able to come to a live show for a plethora of reasons were now attending every broadcast.

As much as I delight in reminding folks that "nothing says I love you like cold, hard cash," money is not the only currency in our lives. Sometimes we forget the value of the other currencies available to us, such as time, kindness, compassion, and connection. There have been so many times in my life that I have benefited from the care of people that I met along the way. Now, as so often before, this was going to prove true again.

Around the world, what had started as some obscure flu was now crippling humanity. People were losing their loved ones, homes, and businesses. Nothing like this kind of tragedy had been seen on such a massive scale since the Second World War.

Things weren't quite as dire here in Canada. We don't have hugely dense populations, so it took a while for the pandemic to really get rolling. Regardless, it was very hard to find somewhere to relax, or to just get out of the city. Parks and public recreation facilities were closed. Travel across provinces was restricted. All the federal and provincial campsites were fully booked and had long waiting lists. New restrictions for public health were coming in all the time. Businesses were mandated to close or operate at severely limited capacity; many were forced to permanently close their doors. People were dying, but folks hardly knew what to believe or who to trust. Covid fatigue became its own condition.

So, using the connections I made in the community that had grown from "I Love Ruthie," I reached out to people and offered a place to camp in the Moose on my almost half acre property. I held a number of socially distanced campfire sing-alongs and overnight campout gatherings. My daughter had a huge contract to fulfill and left my grandchildren with me for a few weeks of camping. When a dear friend had nowhere to go with her daughter and granddaughter for summer holidays, I was able to offer a safe and spacious retreat for her family. Another woman I knew just needed somewhere quiet to spend a few weekends with her fella, where the noise and bustle of the city wouldn't grind them down. In turn, this availed me a meagre income as well as mental and spiritual sustenance.

The summer soon flew by, filled with gardens and children, friends and music. We supported each other in spite of all our challenges, and though our times together were limited, they were precious. A true outpouring of understanding and creativity was still possible. Had I not developed a connection with everyone online, I would have likely just spent a quiet summer tending to shrubberies, watering tomatoes, and generally going slightly mad from isolation.

The fall, of course, brought the harvest and preserving. My neighbour and I made masses of salsa and canned tomatoes. The weather put an end to outdoor concerts and campers, but my son stayed in the Moose for a number of months and helped me shore up for winter. I had stopped streaming "I Love Ruthie" for a bit during the summer holidays, but now it was time to bring the stream back. The university had made one brave attempt to start student exams, but they were cancelled at the last minute. All music venues were closed and restricted from any live entertainment. Without any more in-person shows and no visitors, I had to go back online if I was going to make it.

While my son was around, I bugged him to teach me how to use as many of the social media and streaming platforms as he could. Eventually, he became a little frustrated with me – every time he would step inside the house from the Moose, I would have another question for him. Finally, he directed me to tutorials on YouTube. I mustered a YouTube channel for "I Love Ruthie" and even somehow managed to salvage a channel that I had started years ago. I am now on Instagram, Twitter, Facebook, YouTube, Restream, Islands in the Stream, and Birds Flying Past Your Face. No, wait, those last two may just be flashbacks from the '80s. This whole thing does get to be a little bit much. The point is that in spite of my resistance and challenges, I AM learning.

A few weeks back, there was a virtual International Folk Festival and Music Industry Conference for which I was invited to perform in the official Alberta showcase. Normally this event would entail hundreds of people from around the world descending on a single location to network, perform music, and find new opportunities. This year, the organizers had the unprecedented task of doing this all online. It took many emails with multiple platforms to register and accommodate all the showcases and attendees. I found it to be quite overwhelming, but I figured out how to get my profile built and do everything necessary to be ready for the conference. I noticed that a number of the other artists and presenters, some of whom were significantly more advanced in their careers than I, had not been able to navigate this. So, I communicated with them and helped as many as I could, especially the women I knew from around the music scene.

In the music business, the gender gap is massive and sometimes very unfair. As I have been learning and growing in this new paradigm, I have discovered that I am determined to help as many women artists as I can. Difficult though it may be to understand the digital world, we have the opportunity to thrive. Whether or not this is the new normal, technology is a window to the entire world, and it does not see gender. With Internet access, some determination, and a strong creative drive, women from around the globe can connect with each other. Community is not lost; it is just growing a new branch on the tree.

Right now, almost every opportunity that I am exploring has come from my internet networking. In fact, for any of these opportunities to flourish, I MUST have a strong online presence. It is challenging to learn this new e-world, but I am making progress. Every new system that I learn or platform that I master is another step towards sustainability and freedom. And throughout it all, I am assisted by my community of Beings who care. Although we may be physically apart, these changing times and technologies are bringing us ever closer together and our connection seems to evolve every minute. The digital world is reaching far and wide into all the expanses of human endeavour, and the foundation for the entirety of this must be love. We are finding a new way in the new day, and we are doing it together.

About Ruth Purves Smith

A Prairie girl from Calgary, Ruth Purves Smith grew up travelling the dusty highways between two cultures: her urban life in the city and the artisan's dream of a circa 1800s rural woollen mill. From these beginnings, Ruth found her voice to become an accomplished songwriter and performer. Her music spans the spectrum from country through to Celtic-infused folk rock. Both of her albums (*Out in the Storm* and *Faster than the Speed of Dark*) have garnered international attention and enthusiastic reviews.

Having toured much of North America and the UK, Ruth has settled back in Alberta's farm belt to compose music, complete a new album, write a children's book, develop her fibre arts, and build community around creating art and sharing knowledge of sustainable lifestyles. This is her first published prose.

www.ruthpurvessmith.com
Facebook: Ruth Purves Smith
Instagram: @ruthpurvessmith
Twitter: @ruthpurvessmit

15

Letting in the Light

By Allyson Roberts

"Emotional pain is not something that should be hidden away and never spoken about. There is truth in your pain, there is growth in your pain, but only if it's first brought out into the open."

Steve Aitchison

Letting in the Light

By Allyson Roberts

I wasn't sure how I knew to get in the car and start driving, but the feeling was too strong to ignore. Before I knew it, I was an hour and a half into my journey to the past. COVID-19 had put us in full lockdown, so my car was the only one on what is normally a congested highway. It was surreal.

Driving is one of the ways I process things, and there was so much to process – so many storms hitting all at once. This new virus was impacting everyone all over the world, including two friends who caught it and died back-to-back. One was struggling with cancer, the other diabetes, but still. In the midst of that chaos, I discovered that one of my sisters and her husband are deep into QAnon, another friend was burned badly at a Black Lives Matter protest, and I'd just ended my relationships with business partners who didn't have my best interests at heart. It was almost too much to handle. So, I found myself in my car, listening to music with tears streaming down my face.

I started out with no destination in mind, but suddenly I knew exactly where I was headed. My heart was heavy and filled with anticipation all in the same beat. It had been years since I'd driven to our special place. Without an exact address to place in my Waze app, I simply followed my keen sense of direction. After only two missed turns, there I was.

It was exactly one year ago to this day that I last found my way to this field, where Dad and I had spent so many precious moments together. I slowly climbed out of my car and stood in the middle of the gravel road. With the mountains to my right and green fields to my left, the first signs of spring were blooming everywhere. I closed my eyes and allowed the breeze to wash over me.

Just eighteen months prior, my dad succumbed to the poison of liver cancer. What started as an elevated PSA test swiftly became this monster in his body that couldn't be stopped. After falling during his annual deer hunting retreat and lying in the dark for hours, he was humiliated and defeated. He went home, climbed into bed, and willed himself to die only fifteen days later.

The thing is, we hadn't spoken in three years.

Five years before my father's death, my brother came to me broken. He'd lost everything, including his marriage, and he needed me to put him back together again. It's what I did. So, begrudgingly, I stepped away from own business, poured my heart and soul into a wine bar that my brother managed, and two years later my brother forged my name on some documents and sold the business from under me. I lost one hundred thousand dollars before I knew what was happening.

In my father's usual style – a side effect of tremendous guilt he felt about not protecting my siblings and I, especially my brother, from our mother's insanity – he always sided with him. This time, however, I couldn't let it go. As a result, my father and I were at odds. To make things worse, my brother and oldest sister wouldn't allow me to see my father on his death bed. I didn't get to say goodbye to him. It was pure hell.

Standing in the gravel road, feeling the weight of the world, I suddenly sensed my father's hand on my shoulder. I can't explain it, but he was there. I could feel him, sense him, smell him, and hear him. "Allyson, I love you. I'm proud of you. Nothing is or ever was your fault."

Before I realized what was happening, this deep sob surfaced from somewhere inside of me. I literally couldn't breathe. I dropped to my knees uncontrollably and just allowed the buried pain from our past – when he left, when he remarried, when he didn't call for years, when he didn't answer my calls, all of it – to come out of me and into this broken world. My entire body was convulsing, and I felt as if I was standing on the outside of my life witnessing a rebirth of some nature. I didn't understand it. I'd never experienced anything like it before, and I hope I never do again.

It took awhile before I felt okay to drive. Once I was inside my car, I wasn't even sure where to go. All I knew was that something ugly and disempowering was gone. This thing that had taken hold of me long ago, guided me to make decisions that weren't intuitive or inspired, and took me down paths of brokenness and despair was no longer inside of me.

Holding the steering wheel, I again heard my father. "Things will be different now. You'll see."

As a mindset coach, I know the importance of our thoughts and how our beliefs shape our world. What we tell ourselves becomes the story we relive over and over. What we want can't happen if we don't truly possess the power to live it *before* we experience it. I know all of this. I'd also had some false wins – some amazing things that had shown up in my life before that day. I'd shared stages with incredible women and been featured on magazines, newspapers, and nationally and internationally syndicated shows. Even with all those recognitions and rewards, something was always missing.

Driving home, I breathed differently. I felt lighter. I noticed that I didn't want the radio playing; I drove in complete silence for three hours. My car was still one of the only ones on the highway, which made the drive home all the more peaceful.

The next day, I began a virtual launch for my coaching program. Before the first class was even finished, eleven women emailed or texted me saying they wanted in. That had never happened before. By the end of the launch, I had thirty new women in my six-month coaching program. The material was the same, the worksheets were the same, the script was the same, and the offer was the same. I launched that week the way I'd launched dozens of times before. The difference was me.

As a cognitive behavioural expert, I teach the power of the mind. It is our mindset that makes our reality, for better or worse. With that being said, I know that our emotions drive our lives. We live out what we believe through either trying to avoid pain or seek pleasure, and this drive is so insidious that we often don't even realize what we are doing. We wake up, we go through the routine, we go to sleep, and then we start all over again. Even our greatest pain can become such a consistent part of our daily lives that any alteration, however wonderful, can be hard to attain because it doesn't feel familiar. Without discipline and commitment, we will always go back to what we know instead of what we truly desire.

Do you ever wake up and ask yourself, "How did I end up here, again?" It's a question that I answer daily for my clients. We so desperately want self-work to be a one-shot experience; we want our quick fix so that we can move on. The truth is, we carry our parents' stories, and their parents' stories, and so on until we don't anymore. The only way to live our own story is through exploring what we believe and what we don't. We have to get real, take chances on ourselves, and boldly face the roles we are playing that keep us small, stuck, and in lack.

One of my favourite analogies about mindset work is that it's like our laundry – it never ends. This is because our thoughts are stuck in neuropathways we've developed since before we were born. We have family patterns, stories, belief systems, and behaviours that we've carried around our entire lives. We are literally carbon copies of generations of experiences. We are born into our religion, social status, money story, educational systems, the list goes on. We are told how we are supposed to feel about everything. We are taught to hate or love; to accept or deny; to dance or sit down. Our parents can only do their best with what they know. This is why, as adults, it's crucial to reparent ourselves if needed – so many of my clients appreciate this part of my work.

It's no one's fault. Simply put, it's our most primitive state of being. It's how we were accepted into the tribe. Rejection used to mean literal death, so you can see how our lower brain, also known as our subconscious brain, fights for survival. When we grow to understand this, we begin to understand that we are not victims of anyone or anything – we are merely copies of what has worked (or not worked) for other people before us. It's all based on the deepest primal feeling of fear.

We can't heal our pain until we allow it to come to the surface, and that's exactly what happened on that gravel road with the soul experience of my dad. Everything that I'd shoved down for years was sitting there, waiting for me. Things I thought I'd already worked on. Things I thought were completely healed. Doesn't that feel so familiar?

Another layer of my old pain was waiting for me to not care what people think anymore. It was waiting on me to be willing to hurt even deeper. It was waiting on me to be willing to admit *again* that I'm not perfect, and that I make mistakes. It was waiting on me to admit *one more time* that I played a part in the failure of my relationship with my father. It was waiting on my heart to accept that it needed to break *even wider* in order to expand. You see, my friend, the work never ends – instead, it grows.

At one time in my life, I thought I could heal by spiritually bypassing it all. I thought I could heal by eliminating toxic people from my life. I thought I could heal by not creating messes and running away before things got too ugly. I thought I could heal by taking the higher road and not confronting things. I thought I could heal by saying mantras, meditating, and burning sage. This is called "throwing action at the problem," and it's a huge mistake all of us make when we are desperately trying to make things feel right again. We truly believe that if we do something, anything, we can make it all better. What I teach is a totally different method, and it works! I love this approach so much because I've committed to being my own best student and doing the work daily. Yep, you read that correctly, I do my personalized science every single day. For me, it's like brushing my teeth. I won't miss it.

You may be wondering, what is "personalized science"? It's what I call my process of combining science and spirituality. As a cognitive behavioural expert, I've come to realize that science isn't enough. To truly make the changes necessary to improve our lives, we also need some belief or understanding in God or a higher energy to help us understand quantum physics. When we feel expanded, we are creating a higher energy level for ourselves – and when we do that, we are attracting more of what we want. The opposite is also true. When we focus on what we don't want and how awful it makes us feel, then we get a result that makes us feel bad.

The first step to all healing is awareness; it's ninety percent of the cure. This is because we can't heal what we aren't willing to see. We can't heal what we refuse to accept is broken. So, the best message I can offer in all of this is to accept every part of your path. Get over the fear of what's on the other side and just look at each story with a knowing that everything happens for a reason. Everything we endure is a puzzle piece to our beautiful story.

Revisiting the grove wasn't just about going to a place, it was reclaiming something my dad and I held so precious, which was one another. Our story is complicated and deep, but it's our story and something no one can ever take from us. What he reminded me of that day is that I have a spirit to help people – I always have – but first, I had to help myself. I was reminded that love is the strongest antidote, and that I needed to pour more of the love I was withholding from myself into me. While it's okay for us to give a lot of ourselves to others, he reminded me that if my vessel is empty, my family, friends, and clients suffer too. This was a strong message coming from him because my dad never put himself first in a healthy way. Instead, he escaped a lot. This looked like selfishness to everyone else, but in truth he was struggling to cope his entire life.

My dad gave me three amazing gifts. The first is his gift of entrepreneurship. He built a business from the ground up in a place he'd never been before, and one of his first loyal customers was country singer, actress, and author Trisha Yearwood. Witnessing his gumption to stand on his own instead of working for his wealthy brother showed me that the "easy" way is often not the most fulfilling. My dad worked well into his seventies after having built a loyal following of clients who were also his friends.

The second gift is self-respect. My dad always asked me tough questions and demanded the truth; he used to tell me that he couldn't help me if I wasn't honest with him. I loved that so much because it's become something I tell my clients regularly, and it's changed their lives.

The third is forgiveness. Even though he is physically gone, my dad has sent many messages letting me know that he has forgiven me, and that he's welcomed my forgiving him. Because of him, I no longer carry shame and guilt to the degree that I once did. They don't rule my day and destroy my dreams. In fact, going through the deep healing process of releasing shame and guilt has allowed me to shine brighter and help people in amazing ways so that they, too, can shine the way they are meant to.

We can't be our brightest self when we are stuck in our pain. In my coaching programs, we examine the three barriers that stand in every person's way: "I can't," "It's too hard," and "I don't know how." These lies shape the path of procrastination, frustration, and failure. They whisper to us in a multitude of ways, convincing us that we can't thrive because the path to our advancement is too hard – and that even if it were easy, we wouldn't know how to get there.

Once we overcome these barriers and are willing to continue the work of changing this language, we literally can accomplish so much more in our lives. I see my clients do it every day. They train themselves to think differently and create new beliefs, which leads each and everyone of them to exciting and fulfilling outcomes that would not be possible without the process of personalized science.

If you find yourself asking, "How did I end up here, again," on a regular basis – creating debt even after you've paid it off, gaining the weight back after you've worked so hard to lose it, messing up relationships by being too needy – then you need to do these three things. First, take a serious inventory of your life. Look around and make a conscious effort to see what is and isn't working. Second, take a long look at yourself. See where you are hiding pain or trying to be perfect so that others will love you. Third, get into coaching or therapy where an outsider can see your blind spots and help you navigate through your journey in a way that is completely different from anything you've previously attempted. You have amazing power inside of you, and if you are committed to learning how to change the way you view the world and allow Universal light into your experience, you will be amazed at what you can achieve.

About Allyson Roberts

Allyson Roberts knows what it takes to make it in this world. As a young woman who found herself homeless, pregnant, and forced to live in her car, she turned to the writing of Napoleon Hill for comfort and guidance. Little did she know then what a huge impact his philosophies would have on her life.

Allyson knows the importance of being the boss of our brain while also tapping into our soul power, which is our connection to the Divine. In the past twenty years, she has coached thousands of women all over the world, helping them step into their innate power through a process she calls personalized science. She runs a successful coaching program, Unapologetic Power, which is a six-month commitment with hands-on attention and assistance. She believes that spending time face-to-face with clients is important for their growth and success, and she offers several classes per week to ensure that her clients are progressing.

Allyson has appeared in hundreds of publications, on podcasts, and on both live and virtual stages nationally and internationally. Her expertise along with her clients' phenomenal metamorphoses around prosperity, professional transformations, and personal development won her recognition by Feedspot in their "Top 100 Coaches in the World."

www.allysonroberts.com • www.behindthepowerevent.com
Facebook: Outrageous Results   **Email**: allyson@allysonroberts.com

16

Restart, Pivot, Reset: Finding Home Again

By Kellie Wesley

"Perhaps that is where our choice lies – in determining how we will meet the inevitable end of things, and how we will greet each new beginning."

Elena K. Arnold

Chapter 16

Restart, Pivot, Reset:
Finding Home Again

By Kellie Wesley

Home and family have always been the most important aspects of my life – that I am living my dream of being an interior designer is the cherry on top. I had no idea that my career would save me from the most heartbreaking year of my life, or that helping other women and clients focus on their own homes would be the beginning of my own healing journey.

I have wanted to be an interior designer since I was a young girl. In my early years, I would constantly rearrange my bedroom and paint the walls. I would also furnish and arrange Barbie doll houses for my sister and friends; I wasn't as keen on playing with the dolls as I was about setting up and decorating their homes.

In my senior year of high school, I won a small scholarship to the University of Oregon for journalism. I've always loved to write, but art and design are my passions. I started taking interior design courses while I was at university, and I loved them! However, a car accident in 1979 put an end to my college days. The recovery was long and arduous, and I had to reset and focus on paying off the medical bills as well as my student loans. I always knew that I would get back to my passion someday, but I didn't know when that would happen. For now, it was time to pivot.

Life carried on and took many twists and turns. I've had many different careers and jobs along the way – retail management, corporate recruiter/personnel director, caterer, and workroom manager to name a few. I've lived in Portland, Oregon, where I am from; Redmond, Oregon; Atlanta, Georgia; Cary, North Carolina; and then moved back to Oregon. After my divorce in 2001, I decided it was time for me to pursue my love of interior design. I enrolled in an intensive course in 2002 and finished at the top of my class. By that time, I was engaged to my current husband, whom I had known for over twenty-five years and reconnected with after my return to Oregon. He had three teenage sons and I had two boys in elementary school, so life was busy, hectic, chaotic, and fun.

Our first challenge was completely gutting the home we lived in. My husband owned a late 1960's rancher that had been a rental house for many years, and it showed. We made the decision to renovate this house rather than buying a new one since it was in a good school district and I had the money to complete the renovation. He had started on some of the changes before we were together, but most of those were to the exterior – a new fence, deck, landscaping, and windows. The interior was dark, dated, and old. Working on a remodel tests the best of relationships, yet this one brought us all closer together. The boys pitched in whenever they could, painting their bedrooms, hauling rock out of the backyard, pulling up staples from the floor, and helping to tear down the rotting screened-in porch. Our youngest son, Sean, was in the third grade and was a curious, inquisitive, and funny boy. While demolishing the back porch, we found a skeleton of a cat with a blue collar. Sean took off around the house, and a few minutes later came running back with a shoe box in hand. He began trying to put the dead cat in the box, exclaiming, "This is going to be the BEST show and tell EVER!" We did not let him take the skeleton to school, but we did have a little burial ceremony for the poor cat. It's times like these – the memories, the laughter, the goofy times – that make a house a home.

Going through the process of a true gut and remodel gave me even more determination to pursue a career as a designer. When we were all finished and moved back in, Trevor (our second eldest) came to me and said, "I love living here. I've never lived in such beautiful home. Thank you, Kellie." My heart just melted, and I felt so happy to be able to give them all a beautiful home filled with love. I knew I was on the right track, and that I could make this happen for other people as well.

In January of 2003, I started my design business, Kellie Wesley Interiors. I worked out of an office in a furniture store for a while; it was a good place to start and gave me a clientele to work with. My colleague, Lindsay, also had an office there and was doing very well, so we were able to team up on some big projects. What I love about this business is that it's always changing, and every day is a little bit different. I'm invited into people's personal spaces, and by asking a lot of questions about how the space is used, what their vision is, and what their preferences are in terms of style, colour, texture, pattern, and other elements, I'm able to come up with a design plan that suits their needs and fulfills their vision. Many of my clients also end up becoming my friends, which is just an added bonus.

I was incredibly happy living in Oregon and being close to my siblings, mom, and cousins. My sister and her husband owned a cabin up at Mt. Hood and we had cottages available at the beach, so we were able to spend time with our extended family skiing, hiking, clamming, and just enjoying our time together. Family dinners were full of laughter, jokes, and delicious food. With the renovation of our home, I had room for everyone to come over for dinners, barbeques, and holidays. The boys enjoyed playing hockey with their cousins, and my mom loved watching them play and cheering them on. Life was hectic and crazy but filled with family, fun, and love.

By 2005, my design business was really expanding and had moved out of the furniture store. Then, in April of that year, my husband was offered a coaching position with a prestigious hockey academy in Penticton, BC. Four of us made the move that summer – the older boys were now out of the house – and my career went on hold for a while as I waited to gain permanent residency. I continued to travel back and forth for some time to make sure my Oregon clients were taken care of and the projects I had left behind were completed. And then I kept waiting. And waiting. It took four long years for me to gain residency, during which I stayed current on trends and kept my skills up as best I could. Then, the market crashed in 2009 and no one was hiring designers. Another pivot.

I needed to find something to do, so I started working for a long-time friend in the sportwear, logo, and trophy industry. I was first hired to remerchandise the showroom, but after he observed my work and how I dealt with the customers, he asked me to stay on board. Eventually, he convinced me to get the embroidery department up and running again as it had been shut down for many years – it was tough to find someone with this particular skillset. I'm not a skilled sewer and had no idea how to run these machines, but I agreed as it was a chance to work with colour and design again. It also proved to be a great opportunity to meet a lot of interesting clients. On the side, I started to do some colour consultations and furniture rearrangement for friends and was getting referred to others.

In 2015, I was able to switch career paths and re-enter the design field as a window treatment specialist and colour consultant. I was very thankful for the opportunity that my friend had provided me, but I was ready to pursue my passion.

Over the next few years, I slowly worked my way back to my dream job. I loved designing custom draperies, bedding, and window treatments for my clients, and I was able to build a good reputation and a steady stream of business. I stayed with this company for a little over four years and then made the leap back into full design by joining Haute House Design, a high-end boutique design studio that has been in business for twenty years. In 2020, Nadine and I won gold in two interior design categories through the Best of Penticton, which was a huge honour. My dream was coming true.

Little did I know that I was about to be hit with a huge curveball. I wouldn't just have to pivot; it was time for a complete restart.

At the beginning of 2020, Nadine and I were cruising along with a full plate of projects – big ones! Business was booming, and we were so busy that we were just working to keep up and stay on schedule. In the meantime, however, my personal life was coming apart. My husband was depressed, anxious, and had become suicidal. He was overworked and completely exhausted. We were also struggling to keep on top of our finances. I had been working on full commission at my previous company, so there were some months I did not bring very much money home. Sometimes we had to rely on credit to just buy groceries and gas. My income was more consistent with my new job, but we were still just trying to stay afloat and save some money for retirement when the last student loan came due. Something had to give. For the second time, we made the decision to take some of the equity out of our house and pay everything off to give us a fresh start. We had first done this back in 2008 when the market had crashed, I wasn't working, and my ex-husband had stopped paying child support. Now we found ourselves caught in this same situation again. We were both devastated.

Then, in March of 2020, Covid hit and everything shut down – including my husband. Now my focus was on getting him healthy and keeping our finances on track after both of us were laid off. I knew that I would be hired back once the business opened up again, but Blake was unsure if he would and was really struggling with his depression and anxiety. I had to make the difficult decision to take him to the hospital for a mental health check because he was in a downward spiral. I knew he would be terribly angry with me, but I wasn't going to sit there and watch him continue to disintegrate.

I called his doctor and he told me to bring him in for assessment. When we got to the emergency room, he was first assessed by his primary doctor, who determined that my husband was indeed in a mental health crisis. The crisis counsellor was called next. He spoke with Blake for well over an hour and then called me in to talk. It was then decided that Blake would also see the psychiatrist so that we could make a plan to get him back on track, which meant that he would have to stay overnight. I knew he wouldn't like this, but I was too scared to take him home and made sure this was clear to everyone involved. Leaving him there was a relief, but it was also very painful. I knew that he would hate me for it, but his mental wellbeing was more important.

The next morning, I got a call from my husband stating that they were going to release him after we both met with the mental health counsellor. I was unsure whether or not this was too soon, but Blake assured me he had tools in place to help him and would ask for help if he was feeling suicidal again. I still wasn't as sure about this, so I started seeing a counsellor to help me deal with my own anxiety and learn about depression, PTSD, and brain injuries – all conditions my husband suffers from. This was one of the best things I did for both of us.

Life at home was not easy for those first few weeks. My counsellor was stellar with her advice to take things a day at a time, or even just ten minutes at a time. She also encouraged us to start to spend time together just doing small things with the hope we could reconnect. We both had lots of free time since everything was still shut down, so I made sure that we took walks with our dog everyday. We got outside and explored many different hiking trails. We watched movies and prepared meals together. I was really hoping that we could repair our fractured relationship, but only one of us was interested, which doesn't work out very well.

As the shutdowns continued, I stayed in contact with my clients as I did not want to let them down. Many of our workrooms and manufacturing plants were also closed, which meant there were lengthy delays in the delivery of materials and supplies. My main focus was on keeping my clients informed and assuring them that their projects would be completed as soon as possible. Thankfully, they understood. This is when the communication and managing expectations was vital to my business, even more so than before. I had to remain steady and strong not only for my clients, but also for my husband and marriage. I was praying that we could reset and restart.

Throughout the spring and into the summer months, my personal life completely unravelled. My husband decided he wanted to pursue his dream of working in Europe, and I wasn't willing to follow him. Uprooting my life again when my career had so much momentum didn't make sense. Our relationship had also become tense, and as much as I wanted to work on it, he did not. We sold our house, and by the late summer he had moved overseas. Despite the fact we grew apart as a couple, I still think Blake is a wonderful man. Today, he speaks openly about his struggles with mental health in an effort to raise awareness around this issue.

For me, "home" isn't always a place, a house, or a dwelling – it's the people and places you love and whatever means the most to you. But what happens when you lose what you have loved the most? Home truly is where the heart is, only my heart was in tatters. I felt like the rug had been pulled out from underneath me. It was time to rebuild my life – to restructure and figure out what I wanted and needed to create happiness and joy. So, I turned my attention back to my career and my clients. With all the boys grown and living their own lives, it was the first time in many years I had only myself to think about.

Covid has been a blessing and a curse in many ways. Personally, I have seen my business grow exponentially. People are staying home and using the money they would have spent travelling to make their homes beautiful, functional, and comfortable. This has been a blessing for me as it has allowed me to help create a new space, a new sanctuary, for my clients. And in doing so, I have found healing for myself. I had been so caught up in my personal trauma that I benefitted from having something else to focus on.

The time when I truly began my healing process was when I started to think about where I wanted to live. I knew that I would be looking for a smaller, more affordable place for me and my dog, Kate. I wanted this place to be a cozy, comfortable, beautiful home, so I began to design and write down exactly what I was wishing for. I started to dream again, and it brought me so much joy. My new place is still in the planning stages but being able to design something just for me is exciting and fulfils a long-time dream.

The saying "be careful what you wish for" has resonated with me this past year. I had wished for and manifested this fabulous job and career, but then I was designing beautiful homes for clients as my own was falling apart. I had to dig deep and stay focused on the positive aspects of my life in order to bring happiness to the people I worked with. To achieve this, I used meditation, art, writing, reading, and staying fit as well as taking things one day at a time and truly living in the present moment. I knew this journey would be tough, but I also knew that I was tougher, and that I would come out of this even stronger and more resilient.

I am so blessed and grateful to have the opportunity to work with Nadine, and together we are taking our business to the next level. We are moving our shop to a newer, bigger, brighter location, which is both exciting and scary. We have found our niche in this pandemic, which is to offer higher-end and specialty items our clients can't find anywhere else.

Through heartbreak, I have found my own happy place in my career, in my new smaller space, and in my heart. Being adaptable and willing to restart, pivot, and reset my life has given me confidence, freedom, and hope for the future. I have now found my home, and it's exactly where I want to be.

About Kellie Wesley

Kellie Wesley is an interior designer, artist, and writer who currently lives in beautiful Penticton, BC. She has a passion for anything creative, whether it be arranging flowers, entertaining friends and family, setting a beautiful table, painting, or decorating. She is also a nurturer who maintains a positive outlook no matter what life throws her way, and she recently became a Reiki Level 2 practitioner.

In addition to fundraising for cancer research, ALS, mental health, and animal rescue organizations, Kellie is active in fundraising for the Kidney Foundation and donated her kidney to her friend's husband in 2013. She also received the Courage Award from the South Okanagan Women in Need Society that same year.

Hiking the beautiful trails in the Okanagan with her golden retriever, Kate, is a favourite pastime for Kellie. She also enjoys skiing, snowshoeing, biking, fly fishing, yoga, dancing, listening to music, and reading. In addition, she was one of the Honky Tonk Angels for SoCountry Radio, with Dennis Walker as a co-host.

Kellie has two sons, Matthew and Sean, and three bonus sons, Aaron, Trevor and Travis as well as five grandchildren.

Email: kelliewesley@gmail.com
Facebook: Kellie Wesley • **Instagram:** @kelliewesley

17

The Power of Women

By Jennifer Morgan

"Yesterday is gone.
Tomorrow has not yet come.
We have only today.
Let us begin."

Mother Teresa

The Power of Women

By Jennifer Morgan

The sun was shining when I woke up this morning; what an exceptional sight to see. I took full advantage of it and drove to my favourite running trail at Buntzen Lake. It was pure bliss to run through the trees, feeling the wind on my face and life racing through my veins. My mind cleared with the cleaner air and my thoughts raced as quick as my feet pounding the turf trail. Out there, I spoke openly to myself – reminding myself how powerful and beautiful I am, hashing out any issues or concerns I may have, and reflecting on life events that have come and gone. My cheeks were flushed, my hair was wet from sweat, my veins were pumping, and I had never felt so alive.

It's hard to believe that just over one year ago, the world stopped and I was left feeling so completely lost and empty. I fell so far from my seemingly healthy perch that I sank into a deep depression, began self-medicating with marijuana, started sleeping for twelve hours a day, and began to ask myself whether life really was worth living. I knew I needed a strong support system, and I knew I needed that support system to hold me to account for my actions and/or inactions. As a member of the Canadian Armed Forces, we have a very unique "family hierarchy" referred to as a Chain of Command (CoC); every individual is an asset that holds a rank and a position which, when used appropriately, adds to the overall effectiveness of our organization's mission. It is not just our job to ensure the wellbeing of our members, it is our responsibility. Knowing this, I reached out to my supervisors and disclosed how difficult things were becoming. I was never without someone to lean on or to speak with, and there was never a door I couldn't knock on. Keeping my mind focused and having that strong support kept me disciplined and increased my own behavioural self-awareness. It was an incredible comfort to feel how genuine and kind the people in my family were.

I look back now and breathe a sigh of relief that I made it through those struggles and have the rest of my life to look forward to. I have tried to thank those who helped me, but I get the same response from many of them: "you did this Jennifer" or "you did the hard work" or "you deserve it." I realize now that I made the choice to move forward, and the inspiration to do that did not necessarily come from where one would expect. I have finally found a place where I belong, and it is with my Soroptimist Sisters. Soroptimist International (SI) is a global volunteer movement with the goal of transforming the lives of women and girls through education and empowerment. As a member of the Surrey/Delta Charter, we have supported young girls in high schools by funding leadership initiatives such as green projects and young girls leadership clubs. We have multiple awards that young girls and women can apply for and, if selected, could be awarded financial bursaries to assist with their education, their family life, or fulfilling a personal or professional goal. We have provided basic necessities of life for homeless women, sex trade workers, and trafficked women. We have both funded and collected items for single and coupled families struggling to make ends meet. We have provided funding and requested items from food shelters, thrift shops, and other not-for-profit organizations that aim to assist those who fall through the cracks and gaps within our society. These grassroots efforts in our local areas also support efforts to improve the lives of women and young girls around the world. Our club specifically has provided sanitary products to our Soroptimist Sisters in Nairobi while the international organization has gone as far as providing fresh water wells and proper sanitation to communities in third-world countries.

I have grown to love and respect Soroptimists, whether I have met them or not, because it is through volunteerism and giving back to others that I have found peace with the harder parts of my life as well as my hopeful future as a philanthropist. Soroptimists believe in gender equality throughout the world and have a voice every year at the Commission on the Status of Women, a global intergovernmental body that specifically focuses on promoting the equality and empowerment of women throughout the world. Soroptimists are also very vocal in regard to the seventeen Sustainable Development Goals (SDGs) – calls for action for all countries to promote prosperity while protecting the planet. However, it's the members of the chartered club that opened their hearts to me who have been my greatest support. They are never dismissive of my big dreams, instead guiding me to be more selective and focused on one project at a time. They do not judge me when I am incapacitated and unable to follow through with something that I stated I would do, but rather encourage me to pick myself up and try again. They never make me feel like there is something wrong with me; they accept me for who I am.

It was a Soroptimist Sister who brought me into the warm arms of Christine and her Woman Of Worth community. When I first heard Christine speak, I recognized a kindred spirit in her and saw so much of my own passion and love in her presence. I was immediately taken by her story, and I remember feeling so moved that I emailed her the very next day and introduced myself. It has been a blaze of love, encouragement, kindness, and compassion ever since, and I am so much better for it.

The power of a woman cannot be contested. We are caregivers who bring life into the world. We push our own limits and challenge the boundaries society has constructed in order to keep us "in our place." Our resilience and passion can figuratively move mountains. The true power of the human spirit does not depend on how much wealth, prestige, or fame you have – instead, I believe it comes from the support and love of scores of like-minded individuals, regardless of their gender, who are passionate about making positive changes and who wholeheartedly encourage others to do so without an expectation of reward or recognition. When I first started volunteering with Soroptimist and writing for the Woman Of Worth WOW series, I was intimidated by the number of successful women surrounding me. I also found myself very overwhelmed as I had not been exposed to such a powerful group of women before. These women come from all walks of life, and they speak openly about their experiences and the journey they took to get where they are today. Many of them are business savvy, financially secure, well-connected women who work in male-dominated businesses or organizations. I have been given the opportunity to meet these women, to ask for advice or guidance, and most importantly, to just be within their sphere, which has motivated me even more to make my mark on the world. Most of them may be strangers to me, but when I read their stories, I feel connected with them in a way that I cannot necessarily explain in words. Their influence has lit a fire in me, and I want it to burn wild.

I have written in two previous books from the Woman Of Worth series. In them I disclosed and closed some incredibly heavy doors, and I no longer feel the weight of them against my back. Being able to share my story has allowed me to let go. I have found forgiveness that I had not thought possible. I now recognize the beauty within myself, I feel much more confident in my words and actions, and I have chosen to move forward, only looking back to reflect on lessons learned in order to become the woman I was always meant to be.

Some may be asking, "How did you do it? What changed?" I won't pretend that I have all the answers, but there was a post I came across on Facebook one day that describes it best: "Life is hard, choose your hard." I found reconciliation in this post, and I remembered an anger management course that I had taken earlier in my career. I thought the instructor was out of her mind at the time, but I have since drawn from her a suit of armour. She spoke about internal and external stressors, internal being what I have control of in my life and external being what I don't. I have come to the realization that you cannot control another person's thoughts or actions. If you think for one moment about how difficult it could be to abstain from mind-altering substances, consider how difficult it could be to hope that another person would change when they don't want to or feel that they don't need to.

I can't tell you the moment it happened, but I am at the point in my life where people who are negative, unkind, mean, or ignorant are no longer permitted access to my personal life. I no longer allow them to affect my thoughts or emotions. Instead, I surround myself with women who only have the best intentions at heart. I have received advice on everything from bridging the gap between generations to financing a home. I have also found the power to walk away from the table when respect is no longer given.

Another important lesson I've learned has been discovered as I cleared the ashes from the debris, taking from it anything salvageable and relevant to my future. I have discovered a superpower called empathy: the ability to put yourself in other people's shoes, to logically consider what may or may not be happening in other people's lives, and to emotionally minimize the impact their behaviours can have on you. Earlier I spoke of finding forgiveness for those who have hurt or injured me in some way in the past, and it was in part by practicing empathy that I have reached this point. To be clear, it in no way excuses their behaviours or their hurtful and malicious actions towards me, but it does help me to understand people and circumstances much better so that it becomes about them and not myself.

In a way, I believe that other people's negative feelings towards me or you are actually a reflection of their own insecurities and weaknesses. I have had people ostracize me because I place a lot of importance on education and learning, but my educational goals may not even have anything to do with it. When faced with these situations, I now consider such things as their upbringing and what values were placed on education during their childhood. I consider the other person's abilities and whether or not they have diagnosed or undiagnosed learning disabilities. Have they completed high school? Were they provided the resources, mentorship, and assistance they may have needed to prepare for college or university? Perhaps they have their own hurt feelings or insecurities over not being provided with these opportunities, causing emotional transference onto an innocent person who is blind to their past.

In a previous chapter of the WOW series, I placed people in three categories as their true selves develop throughout their lives: becoming the bully, becoming compliant, or becoming an advocate in life. One of my proudest achievements in my life is to know, and for others to know, that I have taken the mess that life has thrown at me, grown from it, and become an advocate for those who have yet to find their voice or whose voice has become dry and harsh from the multitude of life's firestorms.

Becoming an advocate and a person who is not afraid to speak up on behalf of another is such a powerful position to be in, and it is not as unattainable as one might think. A few years ago, I was trying to encourage a recovering alcoholic – someone who had not only been sober for a couple of years, but had also completed her degree in psychology – to take her life experiences and education and work with others who had been through similar struggles. Her response was shocking to me: even after all she had accomplished, she didn't believe that someone with her issues could ever be of help to another person. I still think she would be an incredible life coach, but I could not convince her of this.

In no way is surviving life's difficulties a barrier to becoming an advocate, or even a champion for others to find strength in. You don't need a college or university degree. You don't have to be a certain age to be qualified. You don't need to have access to an abundance of wealth, fame, or connections. Advocacy's strength is in the passion and heart of an individual who faces the world with optimism, faith, belief in themselves, perseverance, and the most incredible amount of stubbornness. I have taken my growing knowledge of empathy and have successfully applied it by adjusting my approach, observing a person's behaviours and addressing them in a manner that will avoid creating any negative undercurrents within the conversation.

For most of my life I felt unseen and misunderstood, and as a result my efforts often came across as over-the-top, aggressive, impossible, or highly improbable. Within me was a drive and a force that refused to quit, and unfortunately it originated from an emotionally unhealthy place: a need to prove others wrong, or at least to prove that I was "good enough." I believed that if I worked hard enough and proved everyone wrong, I would reach my goals and be able to call myself some kind of a success. Over time, this "focus" manifested itself into the development of poor communication skills, assumptive behaviors, and an emotional baseline that was built without self-worth and confidence. It became very apparent that my inability to think logically without emotional interference was becoming an issue; almost every supervisor I'd ever had advised me to "change my approach" towards work situations. This was frustrating at times as it felt unfair that I was working so hard, yet it seemed to matter so little to others.

There have been many occasions in my life when I have admitted that if I hadn't pushed myself so hard, then I wouldn't be where I am today. Rising above my station in society didn't come easy. I felt that if I had not forced the doors open, spoken out of turn, or pushed the limits, then I could have easily found myself falling into the tragic societal norm: incarceration, addictions, and even living on the streets. This is a double-edged sword, though, as the disruptive and somewhat childish behaviours that I did not properly develop blocked me from making the simplest of decisions and accomplishing the simplest of tasks.

This is the part of my chapter where I am encouraged to provide you with my own advice; an opportunity to help you through the dark, twisted alleyways of your emotions with the hope that at least one thing I've said can be added to your already-lengthy collection. I would tell you to be kinder to yourself throughout the process of discovering your true potential. If you're running a trail or walking on a treadmill, your success comes from blowing past the finish line, not how long it took you to finish or whether you walked, jogged, or ran to get there. I have dreamed my whole life of becoming a Commissioned Officer in the Canadian Armed Forces, and although it took me eighteen years to realize this dream, I refused to give up after being turned down so many times. Throughout the disappointment and embarrassment of feeling/being "not good enough," I kept telling myself that if I wanted to pass beyond the limited expectations that were placed on me as a young girl, quitting could not be an option. I felt very much alone, but once I surrounded myself with incredible women who lifted me up, I was able to develop the empathy I needed to improve the way I communicate with my peers. Their support has bolstered my confidence and helped me determine my own value, so I am no longer trying to prove my worth to the world. I would also tell you that anything you're feeling or going through may be your own individual nightmare, but it is not unique to the world as millions of people struggle everyday with very similar feelings. Reach out to a women's organization and get involved, even if it's only showing up for the monthly meetings. It only takes a moment to step out of your comfort zone and, in many situations, life may never be the same once you do.

Being a part of Soroptimist International and the Woman Of Worth series has proven to me that there may be strength in numbers, but there is more strength in the positive like-mindedness of women and the unlimited potential and power it holds. I felt alone and unheard for so long, yet I never have to feel alone again. Being surrounded with such amazing women has helped me grow into a better human being. I have worked very hard to become a woman who is self-aware, confident, and optimistic. I have, for the very first time in my life, been able to not only state that I'm a successful woman, but to also feel it and reflect it in my actions and behaviours. I must admit that I still have my moments of self-doubt and insecurities, which we all do at some point or another, but I have a network of women who can empathize with how I am feeling. And I am absolutely thrilled to see where life takes me next.

www.soroptimistsurrey-delta.org
Email: jennifermorgan926@gmail.com
LinkedIn: Jennifer Morgan

About Jennifer Morgan

Jennifer Morgan currently resides in New Westminster, BC, and is serving in her nineteenth year with the Royal Canadian Navy. She has lived and worked on both Naval coasts, has instructed at the Canadian Forces Leadership and Recruit School in Saint Jean Sur Richelieu, QC, and has recently been commissioned from the ranks. She will begin her training as a Naval Warfare Officer in the fall, with hopes to eventually command a Canadian Warship. She is a strong advocate against bullying, violence against women, racism, and discrimination. She is a supporter of the LGBTQ2+ and BIPOC Community, Black Lives Matter, and reconciliation, and is very welcoming towards newly landed immigrants and/or refugees.

As someone who is unafraid of asking questions or getting the wrong answer, Jennifer is invested in and speaks out for women's rights and gender equality. She is the current Vice-President of Soroptimist International of Surrey/Delta and is excited to be working with such strong, like-minded women with the goal of improving the lives of young girls and women, both at home and around the world. After attending the Commission on the Status of Women in 2018 as a delegate with Soroptimist International, her interests have greatly evolved to include foreign affairs and human rights, especially for those who live without.

18

Driving Change through Community and Connection

By Karen Kobel

*"We delight in the beauty of the butterfly,
but rarely admit the changes
it has gone through to achieve that beauty."*

Maya Angelou

Driving Change through Community and Connection

By Karen Kobel

Recently, we reached a year of knowing what a pandemic is and realizing that nothing in life is certain. As I look back on the year that was, I can see how making our way through it came down to adapting, shifting, updating, and embracing the lesson of slowing down and making time for ourselves and for the people who matter to us. Throughout this historic time, my mission has been to be the certain in an uncertain time, the light in the dark, the joy in the sorrow, and the community that everyone was longing for.

My passions for happiness, community, and movement have pushed me throughout my life. They inspired me to become a dancer, and then to open my own studio where I can provide these outlets to those who are without. Here at Kahlena Movement Studio, this passion is felt the moment you walk through our door. I integrate more than three decades as a dancer with extensive fitness training into unique and inspiring movements, and I am joined by some incredible instructors who use their own skills and experiences to do the same. We offer a wide variety of classes, from Pilates mat and apparatus classes to yoga, meditation, kid's dance, parent and toddler dance and yoga, and pre- and postnatal movement classes. We also host pop-up shop events showcasing local vendors as well as fundraisers that support everything from local initiatives to helping women living with HIV in Kenya. My workouts encourage clients to reach for the discovery of full-body awareness and deeper understanding through the use of their mind, body, and breath.

Obviously, my ability to run my business has been heavily impacted by the pandemic. When everything first shut down, I had to jump into the unknown and trust that I knew what to do and how to do it – although let's be honest, who really had any idea what to do in that moment? But as a dancer, improvisation and confidence are required for any audition or performance. It was fight or flight, sink or swim, now or never. If I wanted to survive this, I had to rapidly learn new skills and respond to the changing circumstances. Being able to demonstrate adaptability in the workplace and in life was the key to the success of my business during this time. Being flexible was so important, even if things didn't go as planned along the way.

Throughout the early months of the pandemic, our classes were solely online. We created Kahlena Moves Online to keep our community together as we learned Zoom and all it had to offer. Then, we brought this sense of community out into the world. There were so many people who needed to keep moving, keep connected, and have some human interaction without masks, especially those who were living in seniors' residences where their families were no longer allowed to visit and their meals were being dropped off at their door. This is when the Kahlena Curbside Crew was created! We danced in the streets of North Vancouver and Vancouver, bringing movement to those who so desperately needed it. We were invited to dance outside people's patios, gardens, and homes, and even at Lions Gate Hospital.

As the world slowly started to open up and restrictions lifted, we were able to resume in-person classes with very restricted numbers. We rolled with this and shifted our class offerings. We asked the community what they needed, and the answer was connection, movement, and community. The mommas spoke up first, and fast! Talk about isolation. Keeping the bubble small meant that moms didn't have a place to go to connect with other parents or to let their babies socialize. I know that doesn't sound like it really would mean a lot, but what we have learned over this past year is that isolation comes with significant health consequences. According to *Insider*, these include depression, poor sleep quality, impaired executive function, accelerated cognitive decline, poor cardiovascular function, and impaired immunity at every stage of life. The moms were calling out for help, for support, and for human connection. You know what I'm about to say: it takes a village to raise a child! This one sentence speaks volumes, and I wanted to make sure the moms knew we were hearing them.

We added a mom and baby yoga class to the schedule, and it filled within an hour of us advertising it on the mom Facebook groups here in North Vancouver. So, we added a second class, and then a third. Soon we were being approached to create these classes for moms and their closest friends as this was the only way they could connect in this new normal of bubble restrictions and social distancing. Kahlena Movement Studio followed all the guidelines laid out by public health to ensure our class sizes were acceptable and allowed for social distancing so that the everyone could feel safe while participating in community, movement, meditation, and human interaction.

Our regular yoga and Pilates classes have been slower to rebuild, with the community patiently waiting for their vaccines. With that said, all of our classes were offered both in studio and on Zoom to ensure that those who weren't comfortable coming in person could still attend.

From April until October, we continued dancing, moving, and stretching with the senior community at Amica Senior Living in North Vancouver, BG Homes in Vancouver, and the Evergreen House at Lions Gate Hospital. We also brought this to family members of our clients who were not able to leave their apartments or houses due to restrictions and fear of contracting Covid. When the rain and cold became too much for the seniors, we switched to dancing once a month for different holidays and special events outside Amica. I also began to reach out personally to the seniors living within my own apartment building to connect in our outdoor common space as many of them were no longer able to go out for their daily activities or coffee shop meet ups. According to the CDC, social isolation significantly increases a person's risk of premature death from all causes – a risk that may rival that of smoking, obesity, and physical inactivity. Social isolation is also associated with about a fifty percent increase in the risk of dementia.

Our efforts to support our community during this challenging time have not gone unnoticed. On March 4, 2020, we celebrated our win as the Favourite Pilates Studio in North Vancouver as voted by the community through the *North Shore News*. A year later, we have had an amazing outpouring of community support and recognition. Kahlena Movement Studio has once again been named Favourite Pilates Studio in North Vancouver and has also been nominated for two Small Business BC Awards: Best Community Impact and Premier People's Choice Awards. It is such an honour for the studio to be recognized for what we are offering our clients and community.

In addition to these business awards, I have also received some personal recognition. I am so grateful to have been nominated for this year's YWCA Women of Distinction Award in the Health and Wellness category and the Community Connection Award – although "grateful" is truly an understatement for how my heart and soul feel to know that my hard work and resiliency during this pandemic have been noticed by such an elite and inspiring foundation. What an honour to be recognized alongside so many amazing women with such incredible accomplishments. I am also grateful to have landed in IMPACT Magazine's Top 10 Fitness Instructors in BC. Just being nominated was amazing, but to land in the Top 10? It's a dream come true! I have been sharing the joy of movement with our community and the world at large more than ever this year, and to be showcased in this magazine that is distributed all across Canada and through such an amazing online platform is absolutely wonderful!

Have you ever not shared your big wins or success stories with people out of fear of how they would respond? Maybe you've even hid parts of stories or played down all the great things happening in your life and business because you were worried about how it might make the other person feel? We don't often share our wins or successes out loud, especially during a pandemic when so many are fighting so hard just to keep their families alive. And even if we do, it's not a very long celebration because our ego jumps in and tells us to stop. But there is a saying that I remember from my kindergarten days, and it goes "sharing is caring." You need to share your success with others as well as the lessons that you have learned – by doing so, you make the world a better place for everyone. I have chosen to share each and every success this year among the darkness, heaviness, and uncertainty we are all facing because I know this will inspire another entrepreneur, go-getter, dream catcher, small business owner, woman, or human not to give up.

Even with all of these highs, the lows still come, and they come fast – just when I think there is some time to breath, another curveball is thrown my way. As I am writing this chapter, case numbers are on the rise again and new variants are taking the stage in this ever-changing improvisation we are living in and navigating through. The movement and fitness industry has been hit terribly hard throughout this year, and we are now being hit again with new restrictions coming in: we are no longer allowed to hold group exercise classes of any kind, not even something relatively stationary like yoga. Meanwhile, working out at a gym is okay, so a person can go sweat it out on a treadmill, then move through the weight machines, go do some free weights, and finish off by stretching on the yoga mats. We have followed the rules time and time again. We have sent in our covid safety plans despite never getting a reply. We have moved machines to make space. We have taped squares on the floor to mark where clients can do yoga, Pilates, and dance. We have made countless calls and sent many, many emails and texts in order to update our clients on the ever-changing rules and restrictions and to find the right ways to keep them moving. And after all this, I received a call from a bylaw officer informing me that someone anonymously reported not only my studio but also several others for running group fitness classes when I most certainly was not. You can imagine the pain my heart and soul felt when I answered the phone only to hear that our studio – a studio of dancers and movers who have been performing and teaching in the streets during a pandemic, volunteering their time to lift up the spirits of those in our community – was in trouble for doing something we weren't. I had to honour every emotion I was feeling in that moment: hurt, disappointed, sad, angry, heartbroken, heavy hearted, upset, let down, disheartened, discouraged, and downright exhausted. You can see why the group fitness industry as a whole has grown tired and is nearing burn out, but we know our clients need us and will support us as much as they can.

At this point, I have grown tired of the word "pivot." In case you're not familiar, in dance a "pivot" is a general classification for turns in which the performer's body rotates about its vertical axis without travelling – in essence, going in circles. The dancer goes forward then back, forward then back, over and over again. Dizzy yet? I know I am. I have made the decision to move forward through the remainder of this pandemic with high kicks, grand jetes, and maybe a little grapevine.

Being a dancer has taught me many things that I have been able to carry forward throughout my life, my career, and this pandemic: persistence, stamina, creativity, interpersonal skills, leadership skills, athleticism, teamwork, motivation, confidence, belief in myself, discipline, adaptability, and most of all, resilience. When the pandemic arrived, it would have been easy to throw up my hands and accept the lot I had been given – to just sit back and wait until I could do what I have always done. Instead, I chose to see this as an opportunity to expand what I offer and connect with people in a way I never have before. I created an outdoor class platform for those in our community who wouldn't normally have access to movement, meditation, and mindfulness. I combated isolation in residential care homes by bringing dance and movement into their streets, patios, gardens, and courtyards, creating significant awareness within the health and wellness community about ways to harness the power and positivity of physical movement. And when obstacle after obstacle knocks me down, I get back up with a flourish and keep on moving. I live my vision in all I do, driven by the knowledge that we are all sensory beings who are intricately connected to our surroundings and to one another. Leading through action, creating positive and sustainable impact through dance and movement, and providing people joy and hope for a better future have been my mission and my passion. I live and lead through my values and beliefs in order to drive positive change, and by doing so, I have touched the lives of so many, both in my community and globally.

At the end of the day, we cannot be afraid of change. Change is not a threat, but an opportunity to step into a new phase, a new chapter, and a new normal. We have a choice in how we live our lives and show up to our daily routines, jobs, families, and community. We have a choice to step into our power and out of our comfort zone in order to move forward rather than staying in the discomfort of change. Today, I wanted to leave you with the thought that it is okay to be scared, sad, and disappointed as well as happy, grateful, and optimistic. Even if we can't control tomorrow, we can control today and how we choose to show up. As C.S. Lewis once said, "You can't go back and change the beginning, but you can start where you are and change the ending."

www.kahlena.com
Email: info@kahlena.com • **Phone:** 778-317-6058
Facebook: Kahlena Movement Studio
Instagram: @kahlenamovement
Twitter: @kahlenamovement

About Karen Kobel

Karen Kobel is a performer, dance/yoga/Pilates instructor, and founder of Kahlena Movement Studio. With a BFA in Dance Performance from East Carolina University, she has been dancing for the past thirty-eight years and teaching for the past twenty-five. She has performed with Mia Michaels, Jay Norman, Lynn Simonson, Marjon Van Grunsven, Katiti King, Tomi Galaska, Peter Grey Terhune Presents, and more.

Karen has been teaching Pilates for seventeen years and dance for the last twenty-six. She is a Simonson certified dance instructor as well as having certifications in CI Training, STOTT Pilates, and Costa Yoga. Her mission is to build a community where people celebrate, support, and connect with each other, and she has brought this out of her studio and into the streets of Vancouver with the Kahlena Curbside Crew.

After returning from Kenya and Uganda in November 2013, where she taught women with HIV Pilates/dance/strength training and listened to their life stories, she realized her life purpose to inspire others – especially women – to find their own voice, just as she did after the past few years of focusing on finding hers. Karen shares her experiences with others in the hopes that it will help them believe that anything and everything is possible!

19

Just Start

By Brittany Hardy

"As you start to walk on the way,
the way appears."

Rumi

Just Start

By Brittany Hardy

"Just start."

That's the advice I always seem to give when asked what my number one tip is for someone trying to get a business off the ground. The conversation always starts with, "Wow, your story intrigues me. I also want to start a business and have the freedom to be with my children, but …" You fill in the rest. Sometimes it's "I don't know how to register a business name," other times it's "my idea has already been done before." Sometimes, it's just plain old, "I want to start a business, but I'm scared. What if I fail?" Are you going to let that stop you?

You always have a choice in every single thing you do. Will you choose to give up solely because you can't see the entire path yet, or will you "just start"? If you can learn anything from me, it's that the path is never clear – until it is.

Fifteen years ago, I found out at twenty years old that I was going to be a single mother. This wasn't exactly what I had envisioned for my life, perhaps because I thought the only way I was going to be accepted was to do things in the "right" order: graduate high school (check), go to university (nope), get a job that pays well (nope), get married to the perfect man (not yet), then have babies (damn, did I already screw up the order?) and live happily ever after building the life of my dreams.

You know that old saying, "If only I knew then what I know now"? That's where I am going with this. If you had told twenty-year-old pregnant, terrified, alone Brittany that thirty-five-year-old Brittany would be successful beyond her wildest dreams and able to help other mothers "just start" and then thrive in their businesses, I would have told you that you were crazy. But now, I can't imagine my life having gone any other way.

I want to share with you my story of how I went from a literally starving single mom to a six-figure entrepreneur and, most importantly, an incredibly fulfilled mother of four. And I want to share a little piece of my journey the only way I know how: as a letter to myself. It's part healing, part empowering, and part journaling, and I hope it will show you how following my own advice to "just start" has brought me to where I am today.

You'll Discover Yourself Along the Way
A Letter to My Younger Self

Dear Brittany,

I know you can't see it now, but you are destined for BIG things. I don't think you'll believe where you're headed, but I'll tell you anyways because I think you need to hear it.

You don't yet understand why life is throwing you curveball after curveball, but you are only ever given what you can handle – and apparently, someone thinks you can handle a lot! People will tell you that they have always been amazed by your resilience and your resourcefulness (a skill that will be the key to your first big break in a job that you would have never seen coming), even though you don't yet know how those traits fit into your life.

I can see you now, staring at your beautiful little baby girl Laycee. (Spoiler alert: you have your hands full with this one, but you're going to have three more!) You are scared beyond words and completely isolated. You're looking around your tiny, windowless basement rental, trying to muster up enough energy to plan your next life move. You don't know how you will pay rent this month, or your phone bill, or your car payment, let alone the upcoming daycare expense. You don't even know how you will eat today; there's no food in the fridge.

You have two mouths to feed: your own, and your baby. You choose her. But I promise you won't be hungry forever. You survive those hard years of not eating for days at a time because you only have enough money to buy formula and baby food. Looking back, you will hardly remember that part of motherhood because you have always shifted gears and found a way to get to the next level. The only difference now is that you're doing it for that precious new life, not just your own.

You constantly remind yourself that "kindness is always the right choice," and you apply this mantra to how you approach co-parenting, as tricky as it is. I'm telling you this because life is going to test you, a lot! Let kindness be the guiding light and driving force behind every decision you make, and remember, there's ALWAYS a choice.

Speaking of choices, you choose to marry a few years later and you have another baby. She is so beautiful as well! You can fight it if you want to, but this marriage will fail. It was not without a purpose, though, because that second beautiful baby girl is there for you and is a companion to her big sister. She will bring together this little family that now feels complete even though you are now a mother on her own ... again.

You're going through minimum wage job after minimum wage job, and it feels like you're getting nowhere. Hang in there! You watch other mothers in your new neighbourhood (which happens to be a subsidized housing complex) accept their situations for what they are. You can't understand why they don't try to break free of their circumstances. But not you, Brittany. You're *driven*, and you're on your way! Something bigger and better is waiting for you, and it's just around the corner.

Don't lose sight of that curiosity and hope, because it's all about to change for you. That "dead-end job" everyone said would never go anywhere will actually be the place you make real connections and meet the couple who will give you your big break. Some people think a "big break" has to be huge, like landing a movie career or coming into money – as if life is just a lottery. But you know that your big break is finding someone who is willing to take a chance on you, and a chance is exactly what you will get!

You will be offered a job in marketing, of all things, which you literally know nothing (or at least you THINK you know nothing) about. You will be hired as a junior marketing assistant at the head office of Canada's largest mortgage company, where you will be responsible for creating, launching, managing, and supporting marketing tools and resources for over two thousand mortgage brokers. You have the best bosses in the entire world, and they inspire you to pay it forward someday, when you're able to. You're doing that now, in your business, but I'll get to that. They teach you about leadership – not in the traditional sense, but by inspiring you to just be a great person (which you already are, just let her shine!). You tell yourself that someday – you don't know when, but someday – you will have your own business, and you will inspire others to just start, keep going, and grow both personally and professionally.

Even if you feel that you still don't quite understand what your purpose is, don't worry. Trust the universe. It has your back.

Once you're on the path to really stepping into your own power, you find love. You now finally understand the advice you were given that by being your best self, you will attract the relationship you actually want. Just like that, you have another baby. (Out of order, again, because you marry when you're pregnant this time. Actually, you were pregnant last time too. No wedding party for you!)

Recovery will be slow after the birth of your son, but it's not a race. It also strengthens your body and mind and primes it for the eventual birth of your fourth baby, but not before suffering a pregnancy loss right after you announce to the world that you will be completing your family. Becoming a mother over and over again gives you the ultimate sense of accomplishment and power, and you are ready to take on new and exciting opportunities as they are presented to you.

In 2014, you start your social media marketing business, Empty Desk Solutions, out of necessity. Your husband makes a career shift, and you're forced to get creative on how you can make ends meet while he works his way back up in rank and pay. Looking back, though, you realize you were actually destined to own your own business, and this was just the universe giving you a not-so-gentle nudge in that direction.

The next four years almost seem like a blur because they are filled with so much excitement: your family expanding, a new home, your dream coming true of investing in rental properties, and so much more!

But then, enter 2020.

This is the year that you will be blessed with another stunning baby girl. Oh, and if you're curious about what it will be like to give birth in 2020, it's NUTS. I mean, the labour and delivery itself is sort of the usual, except everyone will basically be in hazmat gear due to a worldwide pandemic. The crazy part will be the total shift to doing it all alone. The pregnancy will leave you feeling isolated and lonely – gee, that's a familiar feeling for you, isn't it? You aren't allowed to have anyone accompany you to any of the appointments that had been joyous in your previous pregnancies, but you've had that single mother experience already so you're almost at ease with the way it goes this time. Your kids tell you that this baby has the soul of the baby you lost, and you know that belief to be true. You now know you're ready to close the chapter of questioning if you yearn for more babies in your life, and it's time to figure out YOU!

Can you see now how your path is revealing itself?

2020 is a year of discovery. I don't just mean discovery of this novel coronavirus that we will call "Covid," but of human resilience, treatments, vaccines, new ways of doing things, and a completely new way of life. For many, it was a year of self-discovery, and you're right there with the rest of them, back to figuring out what your purpose is and what you're actually supposed to be doing.

You think, *I thought I was there?! Didn't I figure this out already? I have my dream family and business, why do I feel so out of alignment?*

The events that unfold in 2020 make you realize it's time to reconnect with yourself as a woman, and you start to question EVERYTHING!

When people talk about their "why," you are more confused than ever because you feel like you haven't uncovered yours. You know it's there, but you can't figure it out. You will invest more money than you care to admit into programs and coaching to try and discover who you really want to help with your business, but it isn't until you embrace the emotions and take a pause that you will figure it out. 2020 has a way of doing that to everyone – the entire world is on a course to correct how we do this thing called life.

This year, which is filled with pain and suffering for many, also gives us a gift: it gives us time. Time to figure out our next steps, time with our family, time for shifting gears, and ultimately, time for self-reflection and discovery. Some choose to wallow in the current state of the world and be angry that they are forced to stay home and cancel plans, but not you! You see it for what it is: a reset for your soul, and a series of events that will bring you closer to what really matters in life.

People tell you that they "just don't know how you do it." They see a mother running her successful business, homeschooling her happy, healthy children, and enjoying a lovely home life. They can't see that inside those four walls of your home, it's total chaos at times. But you always carry on because you're passionate about both your family AND your business, and you CAN have it all – just not always all at once. Doubts and cloudiness will begin to clear from your mind, and they are replaced by clarity around who you can help and how. Finally!

You learn how to inspire other mothers to start their businesses by sharing your story online, and you finally see how you can use your gifts. You can use the existing skills you have and that you offer in your business to provide a service that will allow them to take back the time with their families they so desperately crave. The very thing you're passionate about – that precious time with your kids that you cannot get back – you can actually give to other moms by using your talents and offering packages that relieve them of a piece of their business.

So, Brittany, I want to tell you this before I sign off:

- Kindness is always the right choice.
- The people who told you that you couldn't or shouldn't have a business will be silenced by your trajectory to success.
- When you think you've got it all figured out, I beg you to stay curious.
- Dream bigger, always.

The inspiration you were looking for the whole time was always within you. No one told you to "just start," but that would have been the only piece of advice you ever needed. Continue to tell others to "just start," because their paths will reveal themselves too.

How does your story end? I've taken you only fifteen years into the future from that frightened twenty-year-old girl to the powerful thirty-five-year-old women, and there's still so much ahead of us. So, let's take our own advice together: dream big and stay curious!

Brittany

PS – You're beautiful and you're brilliant, no one determines your value except for you, and you're worth everything. Your heart is pure and kind. Remember these words always.

I hope my very real and raw letter can inspire you to just start, then keep going! Sometimes the hardest part of getting going is taking those first few steps. And even though my business is now eight years old, I am right there with you, back in the thick of that start-up mode as a result of reinventing how I offer my social media marketing services.

2020 threw us all a bit (or a lot!) of a curveball, but for me it was a blessing in disguise. I was able to discover my purpose and figure out how I can help other moms in business. Through it, I learned that all I truly desired was time with my family.

I had always offered what I thought were ideal social media marketing packages, but the target audience of "any small business owner" just didn't align with my discovery of my true "why." If my "why" is time – more specifically, free time to spend with my family – then I knew I had to flip my entire business on its head and laser in on helping the busy female entrepreneur who is desperate to take her time back too. My social media content marketing packages aren't just designed to help business owners get their message out to the world and create trust, they exist to leverage my unique gifts to give free time back to my clients.

Did you know the average female entrepreneur spends anywhere from six to twenty hours on social media every single week? That's an incredible amount of time! I can't even imagine what our clients in "start-up mode" would do without us freeing them of tens of hours every single week. That's time they can use to make phone calls, build relationships, design new products/services, email customers, and most importantly, spend time with their families.

When you invest in an expert to craft your social media content, you are actually investing in your business AND yourself. Your business reaps the benefits of professional content being created and shared on your behalf, creating credibility and trust among your audience, and you benefit from your newfound free time to do whatever it is that lights you up.

I'm truly ecstatic about what the future holds for your business, life, and impact on the world. But before you can get there, you know what you have to do: just start!

About Brittany Hardy

Brittany Hardy is the owner of Empty Desk Solutions, a boutique social media content marketing agency in Port Coquitlam, B.C. Brittany helps moms free themselves of the never-ending social media marketing tasks in their businesses by providing expert crafted social media content packages. Brittany believes in balancing home life and work and continues to find new and exciting ways to collaborate with, support, and employ other female entrepreneurs so that they too can be at home with their own children.

Running a business has been a life-long goal of Brittany's, and she is proud that 2021 marks her eighth year in business. During this time, she has served over 150 clients across North America. As social media marketing evolves, so does Brittany and her all-female team at Empty Desk Solutions.

Brittany has been a finalist for the Woman Of Worth awards, the Tri-Cities Business Excellence awards, and has been featured in dozens of publications in recent years. In her free time, you can find Brittany entertaining her four children, soaking up the sunshine in her garden, or driving her husband completely crazy with her ambitious dreams.

www.emptydesksolutions.ca
Facebook: Empty Desk Solutions
Twitter: @emptyyourdesk • **LinkedIn:** Brittany Hardy
Instagram: @emptydesksolutions

BECAUSE EVERY WOMAN IS
A WOMAN OF WORTH

Keep Getting WOWed

Join us online for conversations that matter at
WOW TV, a free community service
where thought leaders, bestselling authors, change agents
and celebrities will inspire and empower you:

www.awomanofworth.com/tv

Interested in becoming a contributing author in one of our
collaborative bestselling books? Learn more at:

www.awomanofworth.com/become-an-author

"A Taste of WOW" – Your FREE Book is Waiting

This eBook includes eight chapters:
one from each book in the original WOW Series,
to give you a taste of the
powerful and heartfelt writing of our authors.
Topics include Moms in Business,
Empowered Entrepreneurs, The Power of Collaboration,
Life & Leadership with Soul, Aging With Moxie,
Mental Health Matters,
Thriving Through Turbulent Times, and Pandemic!

Get your free copy of
"A Taste of WOW" here:

www.awomanofworth.com/books

WOW *i*   BECAUSE EVERY WOMAN IS
A WOMAN OF WORTH

About Woman Of Worth WOW Worldwide

Connect. Collaborate. Celebrate. EMPOWER.

WOW is where empowered women join together to make meaningful connections, collaborate for success, build their businesses, laugh and learn, and celebrate their fabulousness. If you're looking for a place where you can belong, with a group of women who will stand beside you and build you up, then this is the place for you. The women who are attracted to WOW are the movers and shakers of the world. They are those who want to make a difference; those who believe in the strength of a community, and those who are wanting and willing to support others, both personally and professionally. We call this "Tribe" and our tribe is amazing. If that sounds like you, take advantage of any of our opportunities and see what all the fuss is about.

www.awomanofworth.com

And be part of our Facebook community at
http://www.facebook.com/aWomanOfWorthWOW